Precision Conducting

Precision Conducting

Seven Disciplines for Excellence in Conducting

Second Edition

Timothy W. Sharp

RogerDean
Publishing Company

A Lorenz Company • www.lorenz.com

Editors: Scott Foss and Kris Kropff
Typesetting: Digital Dynamite, Inc.
Cover Design: Janine Chambers

Roger Dean Publishing Company
A division of The Lorenz Corporation
P.O. Box 802
Dayton, OH 45401-0802
www.lorenz.com

Printed in the United States of America

ISBN: 0-89328-158-1

To Jane and Emma

The musicians Heman, Asaph and Ethan were to sound the bronze cymbals; Zechariah, Aziel, Shemiramoth, Jehiel, Unni, Eliab, Maaseiah and Benaiah were to play the lyres according to alamoth, and Mattithiah, Eliphe-lehu, Mikneiah, Obededom, Jeiel and Azaziah were to play the harps, directing according to sheminith. Kenaniah the head Levite was in charge of the singing; that was his responsibility because he was skillful at it.

– I Chronicles 15: 19-22

Contents

Foreword

Conducting is a language, and as such must be driven by a common set of rules if it is to be understood. Conducting is, however, a gestural language. Like mime or sign language, conducting communicates within a non-verbal context.

Imagine the confusion that would result if a conductor spoke directions and musical interpretations to players and singers during a performance rather than signal them through gestures of the head, face, arms, hands, and full body. Imagine trying to verbally instruct the cellos to *crescendo* while asking the violins to *decrescendo*, and all the while, telling the chorus to enter *forte*. In such a situation the conductor could not speak fast enough to be effective, and the verbal distraction would produce a very non-musical result. Furthermore, instructions would change from measure to measure and verbalization would hinder the preparation necessary for the execution of musical phrasing and inspired performance.

Even within a verbal context, words often fail to communicate the precise intentions of the speaker. Further complicating such verbal exchange, the listener can misunderstand the intended communication of the speaker. This is not to say that conducting is not subject to the same type of misunderstanding. Even when the conductor feels certain that an exact gesture has been delivered, a player or singer may misunderstand the intended cue. Therefore, precision conducting is absolutely necessary in order to accomplish precision performance, even if ample rehearsal time has been allotted to verbally amplify the gestural language.

Gestural conducting is the act of visually preparing and cueing the next musical sound that is to be performed by an ensemble. It is not the act of demonstrating the musical sound of the moment. The effective conductor prepares and signals the sounds that are *just about* to come from the performing players and singers. Once the desired sound is present, a second and simultaneous conducting function of maintaining tempo and monitoring meter takes place. The present instance of sound cannot be changed. That sound can inform the conductor of the musical direction just signaled and warn or confirm the direction of the musical phrase that is to come. Said another way, conducting is the visual preparation for sounds to come.

The conductor develops the skills that determine effectiveness and ultimately lead to the mastery of conducting through seven very important disciplines. The most basic of these disciplines are those of analyzing, internalizing, listening, and hearing. The conductor's mind and ears are the greatest tools in these important skill areas. The process of studying the score, hearing it musically, and understanding and communicating sounds so that a body of players may reproduce them is truly the art of conducting.

This group of initial disciplines is addressed in the following chapters of *Precision Conducting: Seven Disciplines for Excellence in Conducting*:

Chapter 1—Analyzing the Score
Chapter 2—Internalizing the Score
Chapter 3—Marking the Score
Chapter 4—Preparing the Rehearsal
Chapter 5—Rehearsing the Rehearsal

Added to these initial disciplines is interpretation. This aspect of conducting draws upon all of a conductor's knowledge of music theory, sight singing, ear training, music history, and performance practice. More than that, though, a deep and meaningful interpretation of the musical score relies on blending one's knowledge with inspired musicianship, artistry, and life experiences.

The second group of disciplines necessary to develop precision conducting skills involves the actual development of a gestural conducting technique engaging hands, arms, head, eyes, and full body. The physical activity and drama of gestural language, while related to the earlier disciplines, is quite different altogether. It is possible for a brilliant musician to be a poor gestural conductor, and similarly it is possible to teach a non-musician to mimic excellent gestural skills.

This second discipline area, that of the development and refinement of gestural conducting, comprises the later chapters of *Precision Conducting*. Using the analogy of a staged drama, the gestures are viewed as actors on a virtual stage. Within this presentation, the basic gestural skills are divided into an overview and three functional groups:

Chapter 6—Conducting the Score
    Part One: The Drama of Conducting
    Part Two: The Meter/Tempo Function
    Part Three: The Interpretive Function
    Part Four: The Start/Entrance—Stop/Cutoff
      Function

The final discipline in *Precision Conducting* is the research process leading to a good performing or study edition of the musical score.

Chapter 7—Researching the Score

While a valid argument could be made that researching the score is the very first discipline necessary in the conducting process, it is important to note that placing this discipline seventh is not a reflection of importance or primacy. In the end, the disciplines of analysis, internalization, score marking, planning, rehearsing, conducting, and researching must be totally integrated for true artistic conducting to take place.

Precision Conducting: Seven Disciplines for Excellence in Conducting is designed to lead the conductor in a systematic approach to simultaneously mastering the skills necessary to be a successful, effective and precise conductor. All ingredients essential to the preparation and conducting process will be presented, as will exercises and comparative solutions to help in the disciplined study.

Finally, the most effective conductors are also effective teachers, motivators and leaders. The conductor who desires to achieve greatness in the art of conducting must be mindful of these additional aspects of the discipline, and must be just as diligent in pursuing excellence in these leadership areas.

The conductor's primary role is as a teacher.

—George Szell, former director of the Cleveland Symphony Orchestra

Chapter 1: Analyzing the Score

Like any disciplined study, there is no easy method for learning the musical score, and the process begins long before the first rehearsal. The study process needs time for ideas to be discovered, nuanced, debated and molded, and time for aural concepts to take shape and for life experiences to inform and affirm the conductor's musical understanding of the score.

Margaret Hillis, the late director of the Chicago Symphony Chorus, outlines the approach that is absolutely essential when approaching a musical score for the first time. Hillis suggests that during the early process of score study, one should forget about the rehearsal and learn the music first. "When the music is mastered, then the rehearsal can be considered." She adds, "whenever a score must be learned in a hurry, study it very slowly." A target-shooting coach was known to instruct students with similar advice: "If you're in a combat situation, you can't miss fast enough to save your life." A quick overview or survey of a score will not teach anything substantive.

The comprehensive structure framework on which all knowledge of the score hangs is established through the discipline of analysis, the first of the seven disciplines necessary for mastering the skill and art of conducting. It is also the first step in the internalization of the score. (The second discipline of conducting, the internalization process will be studied and practiced in Chapter 2.)

By analytically breaking the score into both its overall form and the smaller motivic components, the conductor begins the process of understanding how the composer originally crafted the musical work. In essence, just as the composer built the composition note by note and measure by measure leading to single and then multi-movements, the conductor decomposes the work in the same way to understand the details that built the overall work. The analysis process involves as detailed a study of the score as the conductor is capable, starting with large observations but leading to small details.

No matter how advanced or limited a conductor's knowledge of music form and music theory may be, he or she must use all available analytical tools to understand the complete structure of the score. This is not an option. Score analysis is an absolutely fundamental discipline necessary to truly know the score.

Score analysis leads to the important practical process and tool called charting, which is essential when preparing large works, as well as critical when preparing smaller compositions. Further, the written analysis chart becomes a significant tool for preparing all future rehearsals.

A completed analysis of the musical score is the crucial starting place in the precision conducting process. The analysis provides the breakdown of the full score into manageable units, and the breakdown of those smaller units into details which will later be internalized by the conductor. Furthermore, the analysis process makes obvious the markings that are necessary for placement in individual parts as well as the full score.

Finally, the written analysis that makes up the full-score and single-movement charts forms the basis of the material that is used to prepare every subsequent rehearsal. The precision conducting process cannot be considered until an analysis of the score has been completed.

The Analysis Process

The analysis process begins by noting the major sections of the score in the full-score chart. After the completion of the full-score chart, it is imperative to analyze, classify, describe, and comprehend each section of the major or multi-movement work in a single-movement chart. This process gives the conductor the understanding necessary for the rest of the analysis and internalization discipline.

Using and adapting the concepts outlined in Jan LaRue's *Guidelines for Style Analysis,*[1] the large dimensions of the full score are charted in the full-score chart, while the middle and smaller dimensions of the individual or single movements are charted in the single-movement analysis chart.

During the process, the conductor will also note the form of the movement—binary, ternary, *sonata allegro, rondo, minuet and trio, fugue,* to name several common examples. Even if these terms are not a part of the conductor's vocabulary, sectional breaks can be noted and charted by any conductor. Formal musical terminology

---

[1] Jan Larue, *Guidelines for Style Analysis* (New York: W. W. Norton and Co., Inc., 1970).

should never be a deterrent to the analysis process. The conductor should use any symbol, wording or term desired to note major sectional shifts in a work.

The written analytical chart is used for all works that do not have multiple movements, such as anthems, songs or incidental works. The single-movement chart is concentrated and detailed, focusing on smaller sections and motivic units. These units may be introductions, phrases, rhythmic sections, or any variety of smaller units within the larger phrase structure.

The conductor's smaller analytical chart will qualify, in musical terms, the specific contribution of each section, instrument, voice, and the like to the whole of the work. After the analysis of each small unit is complete, the foundation has been laid for the internalization process, which, in turn, leads to the preparation of the cues and gestures needed to conduct the entire work. At this point, the conductor is prepared to study issues such as attacks, stops, dynamics, accents, and how smaller units relate to the whole musical work.

During this score analysis and charting process, it is also helpful to involve another musician in the study of the score. Often, by analyzing the score and discussing the analysis with another interested musician (e.g., an associate, accompanist, singer or instrumentalist in the ensemble, or a colleague), insights and connections in the score are shared, leading to a better understanding of the score.

After individual sections are identified in the larger score, the smaller components of melody, phrase, rhythm, harmonic rhythm, key relationship, and other components are studied within and between major sections. Analysis leading to an identification and study process is foundational to score internalization and the subsequent disciplines leading to skills in marking the full score and individual parts.

Charting the Full Score

The activity of charting the full score provides the conductor with a reference sheet for all future rehearsal planning. The chart is a one-page reduction of the important sectional components of the full score discovered in the analysis process. The completed full-score chart gives an at-a-glance overview of the entire work, and is used throughout the study and rehearsal process. Important relationships such as keys, tempo, meter, form, instrumentation, and difficulty level are examples of the elements that are included in a full-score chart.

The chart below is an example of the full-score charting process. This particular chart represents Part I and the "Hallelujah Chorus" from Handel's *Messiah*. Though not a chart of the entire oratorio, this example is offered to demonstrate that the chart is a practical tool, not merely an exercise in the discipline of analysis. It also provides a solid illustration that the charting process is used for the specific performance and the specific mu-

Full-Score Chart
Part I & "Hallelujah Chorus," *Messiah* by G.F. Handel*

Movement Title	Text Source	Diff.	Solo	S	A	T	B	Key(s)	Pg. #	Mvt.	Trumpet	Timpani	Oboe	Bassoon	Violin I	Violin II	Viola	Cello	Bass	Organ	Harpsichord
Overture	Orchestral	D	Orch.					e	3	1	✓	✓	✓	✓	✓	✓	✓	✓	✓	✓	✓
Comfort Ye	Isa 40:1–3	M	Solo			✓		E	7	2					✓	✓	✓	✓	✓		✓
Ev'ry Valley	Isa 40:4	D	Solo			✓		E	10	3					✓	✓	✓	✓			✓
And the Glory	Isa 40:5	E		✓	✓	✓	✓	A	16	4			✓	✓	✓	✓	✓	✓	✓	✓	✓
Thus Saith	Hag 2:6–7, Mal 3:1	M	Solo				✓	d	24	5					✓	✓	✓	✓			✓
But Who May	Mal 3:2	D	Solo				✓	d/F	27	6					✓	✓	✓	✓			✓
And He Shall	Mal 3:3	D		✓	✓	✓	✓	g	36	7					✓	✓	✓	✓	✓	✓	✓
Behold, a Virgin	Isa 7:14, Mat 1:23	E	Solo		✓			D	47	8					✓	✓	✓	✓			✓
O Thou that Tellest	Isa 40:9	E	Solo/Chor.	✓	✓	✓	✓	D	47	9			✓	✓	✓	✓	✓	✓	✓	✓	✓
For Behold Darkness	Isa 60:2–3	E	Solo				✓	b	60	10					✓	✓	✓	✓			✓
The People that Walk	Isa 9:2	M	Solo				✓	b	62	11					✓	✓	✓	✓			✓
For Unto Us a Child	Isa 9:6	D		✓	✓	✓	✓	G	66	12	✓	✓	✓	✓	✓	✓	✓	✓	✓	✓	✓
Pastoral Symphony	Orchestral	E	Orch.					C	77	13					✓	✓	✓	✓			✓
There Were Shepherds	Luke 2:8	E	Solo	✓				C	79	14					✓	✓	✓	✓			✓
And Lo! The Angel	Luke 2:9	E	Solo	✓				F	79	14b					✓	✓	✓	✓			✓
And the Angel Said	Luke 2:10–11	E	Solo	✓				f#	80	15					✓	✓	✓	✓			✓
And Suddenly	Luke 2:13	E	Solo	✓				D	81	16					✓	✓	✓	✓			✓
Glory to God	Luke 2:14	E		✓	✓	✓	✓	D	82	17	✓		✓	✓	✓	✓	✓	✓	✓	✓	✓
Rejoice Greatly	Zec 9:9–10	D	Solo	✓				B♭	87	18					✓	✓	✓	✓			✓
Then Shall the Eyes	Isa 35:5–6	E	Solo		✓			a	94	19					✓	✓	✓	✓			✓
He Shall Feed	Isa 40:11, Mat 11:28–29	M	Duet	✓	✓			F/B♭	94	20					✓	✓	✓	✓			✓
His Yoke is Easy	Mat 11:30	D		✓	✓	✓	✓	B♭	148	21					✓	✓	✓	✓			✓
Hallelujah!	Rev 19:6, 11:15, 19:16	M				✓		D	193	44	✓	✓	✓	✓	✓	✓	✓	✓	✓	✓	✓

*Page numbers correspond to *Messiah* edition published by Roger Dean Publishing Company. Score is item number 65/1001.

sical selection that is being presented, no matter what length or style of music.

Charting a Single Movement

After charting the full score, the conductor is ready to chart the details found in the individual movements. The detailed analysis of all of the units and phrases that combine to build the section or movement is the most important study process in conducting. Each musical unit will suggest a description related to melody, rhythm, harmony, timbre, texture, form, and interpretive elements (dynamics, fermatas, tempo variations, etc.) and, in the case of vocal music, text.

As the score is studied, every piece of information should be mentally noted, if not also charted. The chart will primarily detail all critical information related to a deep-structure knowledge of the music. Many details are given within the first four measures of the composition, including tempo, meter, key, expression, and other interpretive designations. As the music develops, the essence of the building blocks of the composition—the unique features of the composition—as well as the critical changes within the composition will all be charted.

When smaller units are analyzed and then charted, the conductor must determine the musical role that the phrase of each instrument, singer, or section plays within these smaller units, and by extension, the larger composition. This role may be primary, secondary or supporting, or there may be no role at all at a particular moment. The role may be melodic, rhythmic, harmonic, or it may be related to timbre, texture, interpretation, or textual considerations. Furthermore, the role may be significant or less significant. The conductor must make an internal, aural, conceptual decision about not only the contribution of each and every motive and instrument within a section, but about the overall balance and blend of each contributing sound to the whole.

The analysis and preparation of the single-movement chart is central to the score internalization process, and is the foundation for the entire conducting process and for every rehearsal that will follow. It is similar to the full-score chart only in that it breaks down the musical elements found in the score to a one- or two-page description. Unlike the full-score chart, the single-movement chart should be as detailed of an analysis as is possible, intended not for the broad overview, but rather for the comprehensive close-up understanding of the music.

The single-movement chart contains three important elements:

1. An indication of a group of measures that form a unit of study, e.g., "m. 1-4."
2. Analytical facts about the music found in the designated study unit. These statements—the facts found regarding the music within the smaller unit—are the heart of the analysis.
3. Rehearsal considerations dictated by the facts found in the unit indicated. These are your opinions about what the musical facts imply for the rehearsal itself.

In summary, the single-movement chart is a listing of each measure or consecutive measures of a work, from beginning to end, with a prose description of the various characteristics that make up the music, followed by rehearsal problems and implications inherent in the music or anticipated by the conductor.

The single-movement chart example on page 16 is taken from the choral movement "For Unto Us a Child is Born" from Handel's oratorio *Messiah*, music for which is found on pages 5–15. Notice that this chart goes into a more detailed musical analysis than the full-score chart found on page 2. Also notice that the single-movement chart is personal and informal, and that the comments are intended to guide the conductor in a rehearsal related to his or her own musical environment. This is an important characteristic of the single-movement chart because, once again, this is a practical exercise intended to help in the coming conducting disciplines of internalization, marking, and, ultimately, rehearsal and performance.

The significance of this single-movement chart is that in this process the conductor creates a document that becomes a guide to the musical score as well as a rehearsal-planning document. Further, the analysis and rehearsal considerations emphasize musical material that the conductor will want to highlight for the performers. These points are used by the conductor to prepare a performer's marking sheet which is given out with the music at the very first rehearsal.[2] Such a process saves a considerable amount of rehearsal time for the conductor and efficiently prepares the performers.

---

[2] Appendix C includes an example of a performer's marking sheet.

Exercises

Full-Score Chart

Choose a large musical work that is divided into multiple sections or movements (preferably one that you are preparing for an upcoming performance) and make a chart similar to the one shown for *Messiah*. Note that in that example of a full-score chart, movements, text source, difficulty, solos, voicing, keys, page references, movement references, and instrumentation are indicated.

Use columns similar to those found in the *Messiah* example, but be aware that the work you choose to chart may necessitate new categories or columns in order to demonstrate important aspects of the score. Examples of areas that may be uniquely present in some scores include larger issues related to form, spoken drama, rehearsal track numbers, numbers found in alternate scores, number of measures in a movement, durations, emotional intensity ratings, or any number of sections that could be analyzed and added to the full-score chart. Always remember that the point of this chart is to provide an overview of the full work at a glance.

Single-Movement Chart

Chart the score of "Hodie Christus" by Taras Nahirniak found in Appendix B (or another single movement of your choice). Write the single-movement chart and analysis as outlined earlier in the chapter, but be sure to use personal terms and insights in your analysis. For each section in the score that suggests a single musical unit, motive, characteristic, or other differentiating element, first list the measures studied, then, in the middle column, list the musical facts found in those measures. In the third column, list potential concerns, rehearsal problems or other rehearsal insights.[3]

When finished, compare your chart of "Hodie Christus" to the one found in Appendix B or to an analysis completed by a colleague. The charts may or may not be similar, but not to worry, there is no correct single-movement chart. The point of this exercise is to analyze and break the score down into smaller units for the purpose of understanding leading to *an individual's* internalization and rehearsal preparation.

After your analysis is complete, continue the process with another musician. Share your findings with each other, and mark significant realizations in your score.

---

[3] A template can be found in Appendix B.

from *Messiah* (65/1001)

"For unto us a Child is born"

Isaiah 9:6

George Frideric Handel
edited by Leonard Van Camp

Single-Movement Chart Analysis
"For Unto Us A Child Is Born"

Measures	Analysis	Rehearsal Considerations
1–6	Intro/Orchestra Dialogue between upper/middle voices. G Major. $\frac{4}{4}$ meter. *Andante allegro.* **mf** dynamic.	Opening *forte*—balance of orchestra.

7–12	Sopranos introduce theme 1, echoed by
	    orchestra
		Entrance on fifth. Intonation on 2-note
		    phrase. Letter "s" on "us."

12–18	Dialogue on theme 1 (sop./ten.).
	M. 14 begins melisma on theme 1 in
	    soprano.
		Same theme 1 concerns with tenors.
		    Melisma in sopranos—interpretation.
		    Balance of 2 parts.

18–26	Altos enter on theme 1.
	M. 19 Bass enters on theme 1 with melisma
	    variation.
		Theme 1 concerns for alto/bass. Balance of 2
		    sections.

26–32	Theme 2 entrances in T, S, A, B. Dotted 8th/16th figuration. Concludes in homophonic statement.	Marked rhythms. Tuning of parts in m. 30. Tuning "shoulder."
32–37	First homophonic statement (theme 3). Four-part theme.	Dynamics. Accurate cutoffs. Balance in four-part.
37–48	Overlapping fugato of themes 1 & 2. New variation on "unto us." Question/answer m. 47–48.	Balance of 2 themes. Intonation m. 41–42. Dynamics.
49–53	Homophonic statement, 2nd occurrence.	Dynamics. Cutoffs. Four-part balance.
54–66	T, S, B, A entrance on theme 1. Alto has melisma on theme 1.	Alto melisma.
61–67	T, S, A, B theme 2. New variation at end of theme 2.	Marked rhythms. Tuning on new variation.
68–72	Theme 3 homophonic treatment.	Dynamics, cutoffs.

73–79	Theme 1 in duets: T/B theme 1;
	    S/A theme 1 with melisma.
		Intonation and accuracy on 3rds.
		    Cutoffs on "us."

80–84	Theme 2 duets: SA/TB. Dynamics build.	Intonation and accuracy.
85–91	Homophonic theme 3—SATB. Full final statement.	Conclusion/power. Balance and dynamics. Final "c" on "peace."
91–99	Orchestral conclusion. Development of theme 1.	Balance. Inner voices dialogue.

99 measures / G Major / SATB & Orchestra / Isaiah 9:6 / *Andante allegro* / $\frac{4}{4}$ meter / 3 themes

Chapter 2: Internalizing the Score

The conductor's mind and ear are the greatest assets in the important discipline of internalizing the full score. Internalization requires the most intense focus and concentration of the overall process of score preparation, and the internalization process requires hard work as well as extreme concentration, but the end result is worth all of the effort required.

The reward for this approach to learning the score is that once the conductor has analyzed the score and heard the sounds internally, mastery of the score is possible. A score that has been internalized stays in the aural memory. Just as a known object can be visualized mentally, an internalized sound can be auralized mentally.

We have more practice with this discipline in the area of seeing than we do in the area of hearing. We have learned to recognize objects throughout life and can "see" them without having the object present for reference. When it comes to hearing, most of our practice comes through recognizing the timbres of various voices, whether a close friend or relative. This aural image of a particular speaking timbre is what we use to identify a person by their voice before actually seeing the person.

Experiencing the Internalization Process

To understand and experience what internalization means in a musical score, think through a song that you know very well. Hear it in your mind, but do not make any audible sounds. As you hear the song progress mentally you are experiencing the internalization process. If this is difficult at first, sing through a phrase of the song out loud and then think through the next phrase internally. Again, internalization takes place when a sound is accurately heard internally without vocalizing or playing the sound on an instrument.

Now, take the above exercise a little further. Think through the song once again, but this time, hear a chordal accompaniment under the tune. This result is another step closer to the final process of internalizing a musical score.[4]

The process of studying a score, hearing the music internally, and understanding, communicating, and interpreting sounds so that a body of players may repro-

duce them is the beginning of the true art of conducting. After internalizing the score, the conductor is equipped to turn to the disciplines of marking the score, preparing the rehearsal, and finally interpreting the score in rehearsal and performance. At this point, the conductor is able to bring personal musicianship and artistry to conducting, and rehearse and perform his or her own aural vision of the score.

Internalizing the score is not memorizing the score, although memorization may result from the internalization discipline. Internalizing the score is the discipline of mentally developing concepts of sounds found in the score, and hearing these sound concepts internally. This discipline is what conductors mean when they refer to "putting the score in the ear".

As a result of internalizing the score, a musical rehearsal becomes a comparison of the sound that is in the conductor's mind (internalized sounds) to the sounds that are being made in the rehearsal setting by the ensemble (audible sounds). In other words, the conductor matches the sounds learned and formed internally to the actual sounds made by the group of performers during rehearsal or performance.

This process is similar to the sculptor's craft of carving away the raw materials that are not part of the vision of the final sculpture. The conductor is like Michelangelo, chipping at marble in order to carve all that is not the statue *David* away from the final work of art. Similarly, the conductor carves phrases, correct notes and rhythms, proper balance, blend, and all other areas of sound until the sound heard internally is realized externally in the live rehearsal and performance. The conductor has an ideal sound in mind internally, and works to achieve that internalized sound with the responding ensemble.

The internalization discipline includes learning and internalizing correct pitches and rhythms, but also goes far beyond these basic areas of musicianship to include developing an internal concept of tone quality, timbre, balance, blend, phrasing, dynamics, and accents; in short, every aspect of the intended musical sound.

The negative side of the internalization focus is this: if the conductor does not seek or realize an internalized sound prior to rehearsal, any sound that is produced by the performing group could be acceptable to the conductor. In other words, if there is no sound model or

---

[4] Additional exercises for practicing internalization are found at the end of this chapter on pages 19–20.

ideal in the mind of the conductor, the sounds produced by the ensemble are the only point of reference for the conductor. The result can range from wrong pitches and rhythms to poor balance and blend to a mediocre-at-best final rendering of the score.

An equally problematic result of failing to internalize the score prior to the rehearsal is finding oneself in the position of attempting to match rehearsal sounds to what is printed in the score at the moment the sounds are made by the ensemble. Rather than shaping the rehearsal, this situation finds the conductor reacting to immediate sounds and making decisions regarding alternative sounds in the moment. As skilled as a conductor may be at thinking and hearing on one's feet or sight reading, or as experienced as he or she may be in a rehearsal setting, this still is a potential waste of valuable rehearsal time. One has to question whether such a conductor is truly conducting or whether the ensemble is the actual conductor.

In these examples, a conductor who has not internalized an aural vision of the score is placed, at best, in a sight-reading situation. At worst, he or she is simply listening to the ensemble and judging whether or not the sound being produced is good, but not necessarily correct, ideal, or the best interpretation possible.

The Value of the Internalized Rehearsal

Margaret Hillis, the late conductor of the Chicago Symphony Chorus, was fond of having her choruses rehearse using the internalization method. In addition to her own internalization of the score, Maestro Hillis would have individual performers mentally rehearse their own parts during rehearsals. As odd as it may sound, the chorus would sit silently in a rehearsal room and with the metronome ticking or Hillis conducting, the chorus would mentally rehearse the score. The proof of the effectiveness of this process came when the chorus returned to audible rehearsal, which inevitably improved dramatically. Research has demonstrated that imagining something in detail internally can fire the same brain cells that are actually involved in the performance of that activity.

Making Decisions Within the Internalization Process

An analogy can be made between a musical score and a dramatic stage work. The smaller units within the score are like actors, each having a role to play in the overall drama, or in our case the overall musical score. As the conductor analyzes the score and charts each detail and motive, he or she realizes the dramatic musical role each instrument plays in the overall musical presentation. As explored in Chapter 1, this role may

be primary, secondary or supporting, or there may be no role at all at a particular moment. The role may be melodic, rhythmic or harmonic, or it may be related to timbre, texture, interpretation, or textual considerations. Furthermore, the role may be significant or less significant. The internalization discipline helps the conductor predetermine the musical role of each motive and sound in the overall performance.

The conductor must make an internal, aural, conceptual decision about the contribution of each and every instrument and voice involved in a particular section. These decisions run the gamut of musical expression—from the roles of melody, harmony, rhythm, texture and timbre, to how each instrument or voice contributes to the balance and blend within a section and to the overall sound of the work. It is important to realize that while every detail must be attended to, not every aspect of the score is as important as other aspects all of the time. The analysis process leading to score internalization is what helps the conductor determine these varied musical roles.

As was mentioned earlier, the internalization discipline requires extreme concentration on the part of the conductor as well as dedicated practice and conducting experience. This will take time, but remember—each internalized sound helps solidify a foundation on which the next internalized sound can be built. Eventually the conductor develops a large "aural catalog" of internalized sounds—a bank of tones and timbres collected mentally—from which to draw upon with each new conducting challenge.

The axiom to be remembered is that when a sound is internalized, it is really *known* by the conductor. At this stage in the process, he or she is equipped to teach and shape the sounds that are to be produced by the ensemble.

Practicing Internalization

Most musicians have experienced the internalization process at one time or another without actually realizing it was happening. For example, sing the first phrase of "Twinkle, Twinkle, Little Star." After singing the phrase once out loud, think the same phrase internally without making a sound. If you hear the phrase internally, you are experiencing the internalization process. Now, take this exercise a step further and hear the phrase internally but, this time, imagine that an oboe is playing the melody. Repeat this exercise several times, each time hearing a different instrument.

It is helpful to practice the above exercise with a group of musicians. Each musician can alternate singing a phrase of a well-known song, with the next person thinking a phrase, followed by the next singer picking up the singing of the following phrase. This exercise in continuity helps to reinforce the internalization of the song when not being aurally performed.

The internalization process goes further into a musical score by taking every aspect of the score—the notes, musical character, voicing, harmony, orchestration—and recreating the sounds in the mind's ear. When sounds are heard internally, then and only then does the conductor have a gauge with which to judge the sounds that are produced by an ensemble during rehearsal. The rehearsal then becomes a matter of making the sounds in the rehearsal room match the sounds of the score as internalized in the conductor's mind.

The following exercises are helpful for learning the internalization discipline. It is important to work with actual music during these exercises; select a favorite work or refer to the score of "For Unto Us a Child is Born" from *Messiah*, found on page 5, or "Hodie Christus" found in Appendix B.

Learning to Internalize a Score

As one begins to internalize a score, it is wise to start with a line in the music that is comfortable. For example, a tenor may feel more comfortable looking at the tenor line first. A violin player may prefer to look at a part in the string section. From this point of departure, each part is learned individually and then in conjunction with each other part.

At this point in the study process it is important to return to the single-movement analysis chart. It has already led the conductor in a process of breaking down the smaller units of the complete score into more manageable internalization units. Now this chart will serve as a map for internalizing the score. Study what you discovered about each phrase during the analysis process. Each separate unit should be studied and internalized, measure-by-measure, phrase-by-phrase.

Keep in mind that even though this approach to studying and internalizing the score seems slow at first, it is the fastest way to really know the complete score. Remember that the reward for such a disciplined approach is that the score is truly known at the end of this process. At that point, it can be taught and rehearsed confidently with the full ensemble.

Important Points to Remember Regarding Internalization

1. It is the mind, not the body, that is musical.
2. Correct music making is the result of correct musical thinking.
3. Training musicians is first and foremost about developing musical concepts.

4. To produce beautiful sounds, one must know beautiful sounds.
5. Musical training is largely a matter of training the ear and the mind.

Internalization Goals for the Conductor

1. Score accuracy—hearing and producing sounds that are always true to the composer's intentions for the music.
2. Perfect intonation—the state of hearing and sounding in tune, all the time.
3. Perfect rhythm—the state of hearing and being rhythmically accurate.
4. Beautiful tone quality—the best sound for each performer, section, and overall ensemble, which includes a concept of balance and blend.
5. Perfect diction—intelligible sounds without sacrificing tone quality.

Exercises

Internalization Step-by-Step

1. Choose one musical unit or part of a musical phrase discovered in the analysis process and select one line in the unit or phrase. Study the phrase and then attempt to hear it internally.
2. After you have heard the phrase internally, check for accuracy. If accurate, hear it again internally.
3. Now, add a timbre to the phrase (e.g., a voice, a trumpet, an oboe, a violin, etc.). Practice hearing the same line being performed by different instruments or voices.
4. After you have developed some skill at the above exercises, select a second line that occurs simultaneously with the line internalized. While simultaneously thinking through the line internalized earlier, play this new line on a keyboard instrument.
5. Now, sing out loud the second line while simultaneously thinking the internalized line.
6. After you have developed some proficiency at exercises 4 and 5, hear the two lines together.
7. Continue the above process in various combinations. Each time, think and internalize various timbres for each line.
8. As the internalized lines become clearer, add other musical characteristics to the phrase: add additional harmony to the internalized phrase; add dynamics, *crescendos* and *decrescendos* to the internalized lines; begin hearing one line louder than another, and then work to balance the lines internally; internalize various attacks and en-

trances; and vary the tempo of internalized lines and sections.

9. Hear each element included on the single-movement chart.

Additional Exercises for Putting the Sound in the Ear

1. Think every sound. Think each sound placed against another sound in the score. Continue to practice by singing one part while thinking another.

2. Conduct one part while thinking another part.

3. Conduct one rhythm while thinking another rhythm.

4. Conduct in silence, hearing everything internally. Be able to break the silence by singing a part immediately, in tempo, without stopping the flow of the music.

5. Practice telling the virtual players or singers how they fit into the overall musical design (or drama) of the phrase or section.

Chapter 3: Marking the Score

Types of Conductor's Scores

Before considering the discipline of marking a score (and the individual parts from the full score), the conductor should be aware of the four general types of score publications:

1. Full score
2. Miniature (or mini) score
3. Condensed score
4. Piano score

Each type of score shows the music substantially as it appears in the separate parts, but has its own features which serve an important purpose in the score analysis, study and preparation process. In an actual performance, either a full or miniature (mini) score is used when instrumental forces are utilized. If a performance uses only a keyboard instrument with solo or choir, a condensed score or a piano score may be used.

The Full Score

The full score includes all of the parts on one large grand staff, with each instrument and voice part represented on its own line and including indications of key, tempo and dynamics.

One slight, and acceptable, exception is the practice of printing two like instruments, such as the 1st and 3rd Horns, on a single staff. (This is only done in the full score if the separate parts for those instruments are also published in a similar manner.)

The Miniature Score

In this score, instruments that share the same key signature and/or belong to the same family may be combined on the same staff, resulting in fewer staves than there are instruments represented in the music. As the title would suggest, the miniature score is usually much smaller in size than the full score.

The Condensed Score

The condensed score combines instruments in a manner similar to the miniature score, and because all of the parts are shown in concert pitch they may also be grouped by function. Consequently, there are significantly fewer staves in a condensed score than there are instruments represented in the music, and several instruments will be combined on the same staff.

The Piano Score

In this score, the various parts are arranged on a two-line grand staff and in a manner that can be played on a keyboard instrument. In such a score, individual instrument or vocal cues may or may not be identified.

The Choral Octavo

Not traditionally thought of as a score, but worth mentioning in this section, choral music is often printed in a size unique unto choral music: the octavo. Literally "cut eight from a sheet," a single piece is referred to as an octavo.

The Why, What and How of Marking the Score

Markings on the score are made to bring the most important events and changes in the music to the attention of the conductor quickly and concisely. This enables the conductor to devote maximum attention to the performing forces and less time focusing on the printed score. Typically, a score marking highlights significant changes, new entrances, crisis moments, and other unusual occurrences in the score, all of which should be included in the single-movement chart.

As a result of the analysis and internalization discipline, the conductor will know the score very well. However, in a live conducting situation, score markings serve as necessary and helpful reminders of critical details and moments as the music progresses.

A properly marked score alerts the conductor to changes in the music in ways that can help him or her better anticipate the conducting requirements. It is very important to mark only those places that require special attention. *Do not attempt to mark every variation in the score.* This will only confuse the conducting performance. However, do not overlook critical moments of change or significance to the overall performance.[5]

The following is a list of the areas that the conductor will want to consider marking during the highlighting process:

---

[5] A few pages of the author's marked full score of "For Unto Us a Child is Born" are included at the end of this chapter on pages 24–25.

1. Entrances and other critical moments where all must be alert
2. Tempo and meter markings, and changes to either
3. Conducting-pattern changes due to meter changes or subdivisions
4. Phrasing markings and significant cutoffs
5. Dynamic markings to assist balance and drama of the score
6. Anticipated crisis areas, such as tuning of dissonances, unexpected notes, accidentals, difficult rhythms, accents, or *fermatas*
7. Any correction of errors in the score
8. Interpretation highlights, such as *crescendo, decrescendo, ritard,* or *accelerando,* and character changes such as *staccato,* or *marcato*
9. The roadmap—cuts, alternate sections, or repeats
10. Shifting from one significant part to another, or two or more systems on a page
11. Entrances that may otherwise go unnoticed (e.g., cymbal crash, triangle)
12. Unusual dynamics, characters, accents, bowings, or special techniques
13. Standing, sitting, or other extra-musical cues
14. Awkward changes or surprises in the score
15. Moments when the score does not follow the conventional ordering of instruments
16. Large sections of rests

All markings in a borrowed or rented score should be erasable. Further, all markings should be erased before returning the score to the owner. Since most scores are printed in black ink, it is most effective if marks are made in another color. A blue and/or red erasable pencil is ideal, however it should be sufficiently transparent so that the printed notes and signs can still be read even if colored by a blue or red mark.

When marking the score, use broad marks such as those produced by a dull-pointed pencil. Conductors typically invent their own personal markings, but some common examples are listed below:

a. Pattern indication at beginning of sections

b. Cue for entrance or highlight of a single part

c. Cue for entrance or highlight of two or more parts

d. Dynamics—use larger letters

e. *Crescendo* and *Decrescendo*—over each phrase

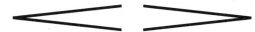

f. Special Effects

g. Two or more systems on a page

h. Next page changes—mark on previous page before turn

i. When the listing does not follow a conventional order

Oboe →
Trumpet →
Piano →

j. Large sections of rests in a part

‖ **20** ‖

k. Alert a sudden change or a surprise

l. Moving from one significant part or line to another

Marking Individual Instrumental Parts

There is an additional step in the score-marking discipline that serves as a vital instruction sheet for the large task of studying, internalizing and understanding the full score: the marking of each of the individual parts. To bypass the study and marking of the individual parts robs the conductor of one of the most helpful tools in learning the full score. Furthermore, it invites disaster to the first full rehearsal. By studying the individual parts and marking them accordingly, the conductor will also discover any errors or variations from the full score.

In the early stages of score study, the conductor will make decisions about various aspects of interpretation for each instrument and family of instruments. He or she will also decide how they relate to the overall balance and blend within a composition (again, all elements that were discovered during the analysis process.) These decisions will include judgments about the following:

1. Attacks and articulation
2. Desired timbre
3. Loudness and softness of each instrument and instrument family as they relate to other instruments
4. Bowing
5. Phrasing and breathing
6. Degree of vibrato

After these elements have been carefully considered, and after the sound ideals have been internalized, then the conductor should mark specific directions related to each of these elements on the individual instrumental parts. It is also at this stage when the conductor must check the individual parts against the full score for possible errors, all of which must be corrected before handing out the individual parts. (It is often a disastrous error to assume that the parts are correct as printed.)

When preparing any score for an orchestra, it is important to go over your interpretation ideas with the concertmaster before the individual parts are marked and distributed to the players. Not only are bowings traditionally the responsibility of the concertmaster, he or she will also be helpful in suggesting appropriate markings for the players.

Performer's Marking Sheet

Because the chorus members all see the same score, one sheet with all the markings should be created and distributed to everyone. Not only does this process save valuable rehearsal time, as each singer is responsible for transferring the markings into his or her own score, it brings an intense awareness of musical expectations to chorus members.

The decisions passed on to the choir will include all of the interpretive elements revealed in the analysis process. These include:

1. Attacks and articulation
2. Timbre or tone
3. Dynamics
4. Phrasing
5. Breathing
6. Pronunciation

A rather simple process, it is nonetheless very efficient and helpful to make this marking sheet early in the study process, particularly while the elements to highlight are fresh in the mind.

Another key to a successful and effective markings sheet is the existence, not to mention accuracy, of measure numbers. While it is common for most published instrumental music to be numbered measure by measure and for rehearsal letters to be placed at significant points throughout the score, this is not true for all choral music. The conductor may request that each singer number his or her measures as soon as the music is distributed. It is, however, preferable for the conductor to see that measures are numbered before the music is distributed.

Not only does this minimize the chance for errors, it also allows the transfer of rehearsal letters or numbers that may be present in a major work to the orchestra or ensemble. Even more importantly, it allows the resolution of any rehearsal letter and/or measure number conflicts between various editions of a major work before the music is distributed to the performers. All in all, this process saves valuable time and avoids confusion in full rehearsals.[6]

Exercises

1. Using a score that has been analyzed, select areas which need special markings and add these to the conductor's score. Begin by using "For Unto Us a Child is Born" on page 5. Then, move to new scores.
2. Study several scores, pointing out markings that need to be highlighted, and offer an explanation as to why these markings need special attention. Practice making all of the markings found on page 22.
3. After analyzing a score, study one instrumental part from the full score separately. Internalize sections of the individual part until the entire part is learned. Hear the part being played internally. Add phrasing and other interpretive dimensions to the internalization process. Then, mark the part in the manner you want the instrumentalist to play it. Finally, transfer these markings to the full score.
4. After analyzing and charting a choral score, prepare a markings sheet for the chorus.
5. Analyze and internalize various instrumental parts from a full score. Choose two or three parts and mark those parts. Go over your markings with an instrumentalist that would play such a part in the ensemble. Solicit their comments regarding your markings.

---

[6] A sample performer's marking sheet can be found in Appendix C.

from *Messiah* (65/1001)
"For unto us a Child is born"

Isaiah 9:6

George Frideric Handel
edited by Leonard Van Camp

Chapter 4: Planning the Rehearsal

After the conductor has analyzed and internalized the score, and marked both it and the individual parts, the actual planning of the rehearsal can take place. As Margaret Hillis stated, "When the music is mastered, then the rehearsal can be considered."

This planning is a direct result of the analysis that began the score-study cycle—specifically the single-movement chart—and the subsequent internalization. Using the list of rehearsal considerations found in the third column of the single-movement chart, the conductor may choose to work through it methodically or skip from similar problem to similar problem. There will be no shortage of rehearsal possibilities if the conductor has carefully analyzed each unit found in the score and anticipated the challenges of the rehearsal.

The analysis becomes a map for the rehearsal, and the sounds that have been internalized become the model or vision for what the conductor will attempt to accomplish in rehearsal. In some instances, the performing ensemble will exceed the expectations of the internalized sound the conductor has determined. Most of the time, however, a rehearsal will have more trouble spots that need to be molded than there is time to do so but, by internalizing the score, the conductor will waste no time in moving quickly to the problems that need to be solved.

In the first discipline, the score-analysis chart illustrated the variety of musical characteristics that could be identified. During the discipline of planning the rehearsal, the analysis chart is studied so as to be certain that all potential rehearsal concerns have been revealed. The rehearsal suggestions are just that—suggestions. It is not necessary to address each and every detail listed on the chart unless the music heard dictates attention to a particular area or unless certain areas need reinforced attention.

The Psychology of the Rehearsal

The dynamics at work in a particular rehearsal are unique to that particular ensemble and to that particular piece of music. For example, the conductor of a group of amateurs may have a different set of concerns than the conductor of a group of professionals. Similarly, a unison composition for choir will have different demands than a choral work that includes orchestra. Even though the rehearsal process itself varies from ensemble to ensemble, some generalizations can be offered for working with ensembles of any size and ability.

Before the Rehearsal

1. Long-range Planning
   a. Outline quarterly or bi–annual projects.
   b. Prepare full-score charts for each major work.
   c. Consider long-range factors that contribute to weekly rehearsals:
      1. Special seasonal emphasis
      2. Holiday emphasis
      3. Special programs
      4. Vacations or breaks
      5. Difficulty of music
2. Preparation
   a. Rehearsal must be well planned and in sequence.
   b. In addition to the rehearsal list, a conductor should know specifically what must be accomplished in each rehearsal.
   c. All music must be ready for the performers ahead of time.
   d. Rehearsal and performance area(s) must be ready and comfortable.
   e. Rehearsals must begin on time, every time.
   f. Rehearsal and markings sheets must be prepared for the performers.
   g. All materials needed by the performers (music, stands, pencils, markings sheets, folders, water, etc.) should be immediately available.

Rehearsal Execution

1. Rehearse the most intense and most difficult music early in the rehearsal.
2. Conversely, rehearse the less tedious and easier music late in the rehearsal.
3. Rehearse the performance at least once in each rehearsal.

Planning Special Events and Programs

1. Plan far in advance.
2. Judge the amount of work involved in the process and plan accordingly.

3. Schedule any extra rehearsals at the same time the program is scheduled.
4. Use extra rehearsals at the beginning of the preparation cycle, not just near the performance.
5. Keep routine rehearsal material in mind when adding special events to the schedule.

Priorities for Every Rehearsal
1. The printed page must be mastered.
   a. Exact attention must be given to rhythms and pitches.
   b. In choral music, vowels must be unified and consonants must be precise.
   c. Harmonies must be carefully tuned.
   d. Attacks and releases must be exact.
2. Interpretive elements must be introduced early in the rehearsal process.
   a. Emphasize interpretation and musical details simultaneously.
   b. Tone, diction, balance, and blend require early awareness by all performers.
   c. A sense of the beauty and drive of the musical work being rehearsed must be captured by all performers.

Pacing the Rehearsal

A well-paced and balanced rehearsal plan considers not only the technical requirements of the music, but also the physical demands that such requirements make on players and singers. It does not matter whether the conductor is working with professionals or amateurs; all human beings become fatigued after being in a rehearsal for a long period of time. Therefore, it is important for the conductor to factor in fatigue in the rehearsal planning process.

Conductors are most eager to rehearse the most difficult passages of a piece of music, but regardless of the specific challenges, if a section is difficult it taxes and ultimately fatigues the players and singers. To attempt such passages when the players or singers are tired, or not yet focused on the task at hand, is to invite disappointment and failure. Instead, it is a good idea to begin and end rehearsals with music that places an easy to moderate demand on the musicians. Placing the most difficult work in the early to middle part of the rehearsal is the most practical placement for a well-paced rehearsal.

Additionally, rehearsal time with a given piece of music will vary greatly. The important consideration is to allow enough rehearsal time to both learn and master the score, which should also bring enough familiarity with the music that the players can enjoy and interpret the final performance with energy and insight.

A Well-Paced Rehearsal
The following is a suggested plan for a well-paced rehearsal:

1. Warm-up and Tuning
   a. An absolutely necessary first step, warming up will help minimize fatigue.
   b. It can be the responsibility of the individual musicians or it can be directed by the conductor.
   c. Other goals include: good intonation and listening, relaxed tone, support, vital sound, range and flexibility, rhythmic training, and ear training; in choral rehearsals, vowel and consonant formation.
2. Familiar Material
   a. Briefly rehearse familiar material, along with material that is not too demanding.
   b. This serves as an extension of the warm-up.
3. New Material and Difficult Material
   a Give careful consideration to the manner in which the music is introduced for best results.
   b. Begin by mastering pitches and rhythms.
   c. Introduce interpretive elements.
   d. Consider allowing time for sectional rehearsals.
4. Polishing of Familiar Material
   a. Recognize fatigue.
   b. Rehearse the performance.

Rehearsal Courtesies
Instrumental

The following is a list of rehearsal courtesies that should be extended to instrumentalists. Please note that it is not a casual list of good ideas, but rather a list of courtesies that is uniformly extended and expected by professional instrumentalists. While this list is specifically intended for instrumental rehearsals, some courtesies listed are appropriate to all rehearsal settings.

1. Prepare the parts as far ahead of the rehearsal as is feasible, making sure to distribute them at least two weeks prior to the rehearsal.
2. For safety, make copies of the parts before distributing them. Destroy copyrighted parts after the performance.
3. Allow appropriate time for tuning in rehearsal, and follow proper tuning protocol.
4. Use the full-score analysis chart to study the instrumentation and determine a rehearsal schedule that allows players to leave when they are no longer needed. This is particularly important when preparing a larger work.
5. Yield to the concertmaster for advice if a technical question comes up in rehearsal.

6. Strictly honor beginning and ending times for rehearsals, and give a complete break according to the concertmaster's or contractor's suggestion. If you anticipate running overtime, budget for this anticipation and work the details out with your contractor in advance of the rehearsal.

7. Designate a restricted room near the rehearsal and/or performance area where instrumentalists can leave their cases and belongings. Make certain to tell the instrumentalists if this room will or will not be secure during the rehearsal and performance.

8. Do not let singers or other individuals walk through or enter the area where the instrumentalists are seated. If the conductor or soloists must enter through the instrumental area, create an aisle that is dedicated to this purpose.

9. Make certain players know where break rooms, water fountains, rest rooms, and other courtesy rooms are located.

Choral

The following is a list of rehearsal courtesies that should be considered when working with choral groups. While these are specifically intended for vocal rehearsals, some courtesies listed are appropriate to all rehearsal settings.

1. Singers are dependent upon not only the voice being warmed up, but also the body being warmed up. This warm-up process should take place before combining the choral group with the instrumental group.

2. Singers are accustomed to reading from a score that contains a reduced accompaniment as well as all of the other vocal parts. Their entrance cues are often visible to them in their own choral scores. When combining vocal ensembles with instrumental ensembles, it is important to keep in mind that all entrance cues are very important to the choral ensemble.

3. Amateur singers are less apt to count throughout a work since many cues are provided in their own choral score. Again, entrance cues are very important to the choral ensemble.

4. Amateur singers hear a complete score less in terms of the sound of the overall work and more in terms of the sound of their own part. Therefore, balance and the sense of the whole work must be emphasized strongly with choral groups.

5. Both vocalists and instrumentalists need water, air, light, and comfortable temperatures to perform well. Have water available in the rehearsal,

and make certain the area is well ventilated, at a comfortable temperature, and well lighted for all the performers.

6. Strictly honor beginning and ending times for rehearsals, and give a complete break. If you anticipate running overtime, budget for this and work the details out in advance of the rehearsal.

7. Make certain that the singers know where break rooms, water fountains, rest rooms, and other courtesy rooms are located.

Additional Considerations

The following considerations will add to your thinking about rehearsal planning after you are well into a rehearsal process:

1. Teach your ensemble something new at every rehearsal.

2. Make every piece of music you rehearse meaningful to the ensemble. Help to uncover and reveal the interpretive elements of the music.

3. Remember that ensembles are made up of individuals.

4. Work to build the ensemble as community.

5. Show the ensemble that you value their time, and that you are determined to make the rehearsal time worthwhile.

6. Keep rehearsals fresh, reinventing the basic rehearsal plan often. Keep the element of discovery alive in each rehearsal.

7. Look for ways to keep communication strong.

8. Prepare everything for every new rehearsal. Do not ever go into a rehearsal unprepared, even if you have rehearsed the same material before.

9. Consider the flow of every rehearsal, always thinking through what you need to do with each piece rehearsed.

10. Plan escape routes if the rehearsal gets bogged down.

11. If the rehearsal becomes too intense, be prepared to lighten the process.

Exercises

1. Plan a rehearsal using the material developed in the third column of the single-movement chart and the outline presented in this chapter.

2. Write out a rehearsal plan and visualize delivering the directions to a performing ensemble. Actually talk through the rehearsal of the musical score as if delivering the instructions to an actual ensemble. (Chapter 5 will further develop this idea of "rehearsing the rehearsal" in your planning and preparation process prior to the rehearsal.)

Chapter 5: Rehearsing the Rehearsal

The rehearsal itself needs to be mentally rehearsed by the thoroughly prepared conductor. This "rehearsal of the rehearsal" may be a novel concept to the conductor, but should be considered an important discipline in the preparation process as it will bring confidence to the conductor, and ultimately to the performing ensemble.

It has been documented that mental rehearsal improves the performance of athletes. In preparation for the 2000 Olympic games, American diver Laura Wilkinson would sit for hours each day on the diving platform, internally rehearsing her detailed vision of each of her performance dives. She eventually won the gold metal in an upset victory in the ten-meter platform competition.[7]

Research has demonstrated that imagining something in detail can fire the same brain cells that are involved in the actual performance of that activity. According to recent neurological studies, during mental rehearsal the brain circuitry moves through its sequence of events, building connections and relationships as if actually experiencing the real event.

To accomplish a mental walk-through of the rehearsal, the conductor will want to both think through the desired sounds as internalized earlier as well as physically conduct through the score. This process will lead to areas in both the score and the conductor's technique that will require special attention during the rehearsal. Such realizations are the ultimate purpose for rehearsing the rehearsal.

This process should follow the outline of the single-movement analysis chart prepared earlier. Each section should be thought through while gestures are conducted. Anticipated problems in each section should be treated as if the conductor is actually speaking to the performers. Illustrations and introductions should also be thought through during this early mental process.

In this discipline, the conductor is internalizing and visualizing not only the music to be rehearsed, but also his or her response to the performing ensemble. This visualization process anticipates the sounds that an ensemble will make as the score progresses. Furthermore, the conductor anticipates a reaction to the sounds made in rehearsal.

While spontaneity is an exciting part of the rehearsal experience, the term planned spontaneity implies a helpful time-saving consideration for the thoughtful conductor. There is ample evidence that most conductors talk entirely too much during the actual rehearsal. Rehearsing the rehearsal ahead of time by completely thinking through the process will help prevent a waste of valuable rehearsal time.

There are several keys to success in preparing the actual rehearsal. Perhaps one of the most significant to remember is that you are working with people, and that people are going to accomplish the musical demands that you are preparing to rehearse. The individual performers need to be taught and inspired. The conductor who desires precise results cannot take this dimension of leadership lightly. The preparation to lead is as demanding a discipline as the others outlined in this book.

The psychological impact of a rehearsal begins long before the players and singers come to the actual rehearsal. The conductor must select music that challenges, inspires and gives positive musical experiences to performers and audiences alike. The rehearsal must be approached with a positive mental attitude and with excitement. The desired results of the rehearsal process must be anticipated by the well-prepared conductor. Such an attitude will best be backed up by careful forethought, planning and personal rehearsing of the rehearsal. If the conductor is confident, the performers will soon follow with good results.

The discipline of rehearsing the rehearsal helps the conductor know exactly what is desired in the rehearsal setting. Such a discipline eliminates dead time in rehearsal, keeping the pace lively and directed. A rehearsed rehearsal moves at a quick pace, keeping performers alert and ready. It proceeds with authority. The conductor is articulate, commanding the best attention of the performers.

Rehearse the Rehearsal Environment

Disciplined surroundings also positively effect the performing ensemble. This includes a clean, well-lighted and well-ventilated rehearsal space. In addition, a

---

[7] Jim Loehr and Tony Schwarz, Harvard Business Review, "The Making of the Corporate Athlete," January 2001.

disciplined environment is neatly arranged, and an organized management system is in place for distributing the materials needed by all participants.

Reacting to the Rehearsal

Immediately at the conclusion of each rehearsal, the conductor begins thinking about the next rehearsal. Note your thoughts and reactions as soon as possible. Many good ideas are lost when they are not written down immediately. This need not be a lengthy notation, but rather, a simple note in the third column of the single-movement analysis chart. These notes should receive serious attention as the next rehearsal is planned. Such a disciplined approach to recording your reactions helps to lock in short-range goals as well as keep in focus the long-term goals.

Further, spend some time thinking through not only the internalized sounds of the musical score, but the actual sounds heard in the rehearsal. Note the differences between the two and add the implications to the rehearsal plan for the coming rehearsal. When a certain approach to a problem does not seem to be working, analyze the musical problem again and think through new approaches to the same problem.

Feedback is a must for the conductor. Without it, it is difficult to get a clear picture of the ensemble's progress. An audio or video recording of the events of a rehearsal is an invaluable source of feedback for the next rehearsal, as are the comments of a colleague. All possible provisions should be made to see that such feedback is available to you. When feedback is given, be prepared to realize the situation, accept what is offered (including any criticisms), analyze the feedback, correct or affirm the direction of the rehearsed passages, and learn from the feedback.

The Best First Rehearsal

There is nothing more exciting—or more frightening—than the first rehearsal, particularly if it is the first rehearsal as the conductor of a new ensemble. Expectations are very high on both the part of the ensemble and the new conductor. And looming in the back of everyone's minds are the inevitable comparisons, the second-guessing, and—not to be underestimated—the very real power of the first impression. To help ensure that things go smoothly, there are a number of rehearsal preparations that should be undertaken.

1. Hand out a complete, detailed rehearsal plan at the start of the first rehearsal.

The purpose of this step is two-fold. Musically, it will allow the ensemble to see what you have thought about, what is important to you, and what details you are going to work on in this rehearsal. Encourage the ensemble to study the plan and mark their parts accordingly.

From a leadership position, it will help show the ensemble that you are an organized person. Disorganization is rarely liked or respected. In fact, nothing undoes a productive rehearsal dynamic like an unorganized leader. In your early rehearsals, organize everything in the rehearsal room that can be organized, and insist that this is your style. Communicate organization. As performers begin talking about you, their conductor, do not be happy until you hear that you are the most organized person they have ever seen. Organization will be your first new friend in this new position.

2. Preplan activities.

Schedule one or two preplanned activities for the first rehearsal. These can include a projected outline of the next program, a short demo of a piece of music you intend to program, or a unique way of making announcements—anything to show the choir that you are in control, that this is your rehearsal.

Your new ensemble needs to be certain you are the authority, and that you intend to kindly use that authority for the good of the ensemble. These activities will show that you are the architect of the rehearsal hour. Your new ensemble will learn to like you in time, and they will find you interesting at the first rehearsal. But what they really want to know is that you are in charge and that you are going to bring leadership to the ensemble. Your greatest hope for the first rehearsal is to know the music better than anyone in the room so that you can personify leadership first with the music, and then with the overall time spent in the rehearsal.

3. Do not do anything in the rehearsal that is not written out for the ensemble.

Hand materials out, use an overhead, have lists on the wall—any written method of communication that is available to you. Your goal is to demonstrate as many layers of written communication as possible, making the ensemble believe you are a superb communicator.

Discover the traditions, the logistic requirements for performances, and any other routines that the ensemble is accustomed to, and *write them down*. Post them on an announcement board; you can tell the ensemble that you want all newcomers to be familiar with these procedures, although they are really for the veterans and for you as well. Verbal announcements are okay, but be sure that they are also written down on the rehearsal sheet. If you have the next performance list ready, hand it out to the ensemble during the rehearsal. All of this will demonstrate to the ensemble how much you care about communication.

4. Memorize the score.

We only look at the music when we are not secure and do not remember what is on the page. Therefore, every time we look at the page, we communicate insecurity to the choir, no matter how subtle the look is. In contrast, if you never look down, you may never communicate insecurity. This is your desire for your first rehearsal.

Be able to look your ensemble members in the eye as you convey your passion for the music. Be prepared, demonstrate that you are prepared, and build the trust of the ensemble as someone who is prepared and wants to communicate. Furthermore, if ever you do begin to feel insecure, your passion for and knowledge of the music will be your friend during the rehearsal process.

5. Adhere to the rehearsal sheet.

The rehearsal sheet brings another level of authority to the rehearsal. Working through it will show an ensemble that you are calm and ordered, and that this order is something that they too can calmly anticipate. It also demonstrates careful planning. In time, the careful planning and execution on your part will keep the ensemble from worrying about future performances.

This will also enable you to remind the ensemble to look ahead and mark and study areas in the music that are coming. Try not to give instructions that were not analyzed ahead of time or included on your rehearsal sheet. There is something about having these markings and musical desires written down that will keep anyone from saying, "we didn't do it that way before."

6. Affirm the ensemble's history.

Always be positive and affirming about your ensemble's recent past. If you talk about any conversations between you and an ensemble's previous director, be positive. Work to show the ensemble that now that you are with them, their history is a part of your history. Do not be afraid of it, but rather, acknowledge and talk about it, and celebrate it with the ensemble. They should feel comfortable reliving their history with you, and you can start the process by taking the first step in the first rehearsal.

7. Planned spontaneity.

Plan one surprise in the rehearsal to show the ensemble what they can look forward to each week as a part of your style of leadership. For example: introduce your family to the ensemble; do something comical that no one knows you can do; give away fast-food or ice cream coupons to everyone that was on time; read a note from a former director that introduces you to the ensemble.

One such activity I planned was to read a message from the composer of one of the pieces that we were rehearsing. This was surprisingly simple to achieve. I simply faxed a note to the composer asking for a few words about the piece that we were rehearsing. It was no problem for him to send a few sentences back to me by fax. During the first rehearsal, I told the ensemble what I had done and then read the meaningful words to the ensemble. In addition, I read the salutation of the fax, which was personally addressed to the members of that particular ensemble. This surprise proved to be a wonderful moment of planned spontaneity for the ensemble, and enhanced their already quickly growing appreciation of the piece that we were rehearsing.

8. Take still or moving pictures of the ensemble.

Nothing is more important than knowing the names of the performers. In fact, this may be the most important thing that you will do in your first days with your new ensemble. An important tool to help with this task is a camera. If you have a video camera, film everyone saying their names. If you have a traditional camera, take a photograph of the ensemble. To further assist you, have an officer or principal make a seating chart for you. This chart, along with your video (or picture) will give you something to review every day as you prepare for the next rehearsal. This will take you a long way toward knowing the names of your ensemble members the first week.

Show the ensemble your desire to get to know them quickly. Then do it. Nothing will make a greater impression on your new ensemble than for you to go to the next rehearsal and name every person. This will communicate how serious you are about getting to know them, especially if you are working with 100 people. I have made this my top priority in each new setting. People love nothing more than hearing their own name. You cannot let this come slowly over time. If anything needs a proactive and quick-start approach it is the memorization of everyone's names. It will be work, but it is important work.

9. Choose music that is known.

For the first rehearsal, it is important to choose music that you know very well, and it is even better if the ensemble is also familiar with these selections. In this situation, you can communicate clearly with the ensemble and they can be confident in their playing or singing. As you bring new insights to music that they are already secure with, everyone's trust level will rise.

10. Plan music selections carefully and well in advance.

As you build trust with your new ensemble, the music that you choose will be a part of that trust-building work. If you can plan music that the ensemble is familiar with and that you already know in the early weeks of your arrival, everyone will feel more confident. In addition, by choosing music that is both appropriate for the coming season and familiar, you will be able to do all of the above activities with more confidence. Talking to the former director, accompanists, or ensemble officers, leaders, or members will help you discover appropriate selections.

First impressions are very important, and the most important first impression you can give to your new ensemble is that you are a leader, you are knowledgeable, you are prepared, you are organized, you are a communicator, and you are a caring person. These steps will leave no doubt in the minds of the ensemble members that these are your leadership skills and desires.

Exercises

1. Using the rehearsal plan developed in Chapter 4, mentally rehearse a score using both the second column of the single-movement chart as well as the third column of rehearsal considerations. Hear the music internally and anticipate moments of instruction.

2. Repeat the above exercise, this time anticipating rehearsal mistakes and responses you will make to these mistakes.

Chapter 6: Conducting the Score

Part One: The Drama of Conducting

When we think of a staged drama, whether a play, opera, or musical, certain elements come to mind. Actors, stage, curtains, script, director—all are familiar in a list of dramatic terminology.

More specifically, if we think of a stage, we think of stage directions such as up stage, down stage, stage left, and stage right. We think of off-stage areas such as the wings and the orchestra pit. Furthermore, we think of actors working against a backdrop, using and interpreting a script, and presenting the results to an audience.

Many of these elements also apply to the conductor, who works on a virtual stage and can use the dramatic stage as an excellent frame of understanding for studying the gestural language of the conducting art.

Consider the dramatic gestural arenas of the conductor. The conductor's arms, hands, fingers, head, face and, indeed, the conductor's own body "act" with beat patterns and gestures of musicality. All are placed against a backdrop of the trunk of the body. Further, these elements are presented on an imaginary stage, variously described as the *plane of beat*, *point of beat*, and *ictus*. Each refers to the imaginary stage floor that serves as a platform for the gestures of the conductor as he or she silently works out the musical script of the score on this dramatic stage.

The conductor's body backdrop as well as the actors on the stage—the arms, hands, fingers, head, face, and entire body—each have subtle features and rules of operation and perception that add precision to the drama of gestural language in very specific ways. Understanding these rules and practicing toward a precise conducting technique will improve the nonverbal communication that is an absolute must for the effective conductor.

Body Actors Used in Precision Conducting

The arm, as used in precision conducting, divides into upper arm, lower arm, elbow, hand, palm, and fingers. Each division has a place in the lexicon of dramatic gestural language.

The conductor's head, when used as a gestural tool, as well as the specific features of the face, all signal dramatic interpretive gestures. The forehead, eyebrows, and most effectively, one's eyes and mouth are strong tools to be used by the effective conductor.

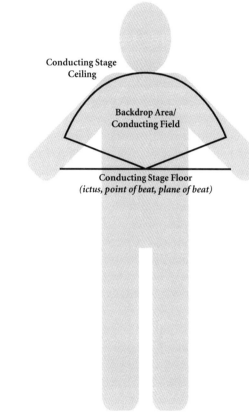

Illustrated Definitions of "Body Actors"

The trunk of the body serves as the backdrop to conducting drama, but it also turns and adjusts in other ways to enhance the conductor's communication. The shoulders, overall posture, and general stance of the conductor, as individual elements and in combination, reflect a leadership attitude and send important signals to your musicians.

The Arms

The arms are the most visually prominent actors on the conducting stage. As such, they perform a significant primary function in the skill of conducting—indicating tempo and meter. In one way or another, many of the great composers, conductors, and performers have commented that if tempo is wrong in a musical work, everything will be wrong. If the conductor does not signal the correct tempo, there is no standard for the musicians to follow.

Conductors fear having their principle function reduced to merely marking time; a glorified metronome, if you will. This is not necessarily a pejorative role for the arms to play.

All of the prompting that must occur for effective conducting must occur within the framework of meter and tempo. Only the conductor signals precisely the changes that are to come from measure to measure. Although it is fair to assume that performers are counting and listening for cues, they cannot know precisely the length of an *allargando* or *fermata*. That is the job of the conductor. Therefore, the Meter/Tempo function of the conductor, as signaled by the arms, should be established as a fundamental element of precise gestural language.

Having established the necessity of the Meter/Tempo function, it should also be established that gestures for tempo and meter are not necessarily of primary importance to the learning of the conducting repertoire. Therefore, as the study of arm gestures begins, meter and tempo will be set aside so that an understanding of the drama of the various conducting gestures can be considered. Like all musical characteristics central to effective conducting, meter and tempo will be introduced in time.

The Hands

If the arms are considered the most significant "actors" in the action of the drama of conducting, the hands are the detailed articulators for the drama. The hands bring a finely tuned accuracy to the visual focus of the performer. It is with the hands that the detail of the cutoff is executed, that interpretive musical characteristics in the initial preparation are signaled, and that various nuances and shadings are gestured throughout the performance.

Although a metronome can provide the basics of meter and tempo, there is no substitute for the role of musical leadership that one can achieve through the area of interpretation. The hands are the key to the subtleties needed to signal these interpretive gestures.

Because the hands are an extension of the arms, they will naturally perform in the Meter/Tempo function. Conversely, the arms are not disconnected from the Interpretive function. The same may be said for the face, shoulders, and entire body backdrop. All of these actors work in coordination with each other toward the final drama of performance.

The Body Backdrop

In a conventional drama, action takes place before a backdrop that helps focus the attention of those watching the drama. In conducting, this function is served by the area of the body from the shoulders to the waistline. This area, more commonly called the trunk of the body, provides the neutral environment and focus necessary for the arms and hands to act out their conducting drama.

The purpose of the neutral environment on which the gestures are acted out is to bring clarity and focus to that which is being communicated by the hands and arms. The face is included in this backdrop, and can be utilized very effectively in the drama of gestural language.

Returning to the analogy of the stage, the acting does not take place off stage in areas such as the wings or the orchestral pit. For focus and therefore effectiveness, the acting takes place on stage. In fact, terms such as center stage, stage left, and stage right all refer to specific locations on stage where the central acting takes place. These specific geographical areas are used for maximum effectiveness in the course of a drama.

The stage analogy is quite appropriate for precision conducing. To achieve maximum visual effectiveness, the drama of gestural conducting is played out on stage. Gestures that are made without the benefit of the body backdrop lose focus for the performers.

In the broadest terms, strong and effective conducting takes place against the backdrop of a neutral body trunk. Weak and ineffective conducting takes place off this visual plane. Conductors that recognize the effectiveness of centered conducting and practice such conducting are more precise conductors.

The Lower Body

The drama of gestural conducting is acted out on a stage, not below the stage. For the very practical reason that the dramatic action cannot be observed when the gestures occur below the waist, conducting is gestured at and above the waistline. This imaginary line forms the stage = floor level. Conventionally, this stage level has been termed the *point of beat*, *plane of beat*, or *ictus* point.

The lower body provides obvious support for the arms, hands, shoulders, and body backdrop. Along with the position of the back, shoulders and head, the lower body provides foundation for the conductor's overall posture.

The ideal position for the lower body is for one foot to be placed slightly in front of the other as if walking, with the weight of the body distributed on both legs. This posture is the most comfortable conducting position, and it is also a more aggressive posture, conveying leadership and control to the performing ensemble. Such posture enhances the visual leadership role of the conductor. Above all, find balance, buoyancy and comfort in your role as conductor/leader.

The Head and Face

Although the head has no backdrop, it is a feature of general focus for performers because of the prominent facial "actors". Also, because we generally focus eye to eye when we communicate verbally, the face is naturally a strong dramatic center.

Within this area, the conductor's eyes are the most effective tool in the gestural language. They can be used to support entrances, preparations, and to interpret aspects of the music. Perhaps their most effective use is to signal cues to specific sections or soloists. The combination of eye contact to a cued section of a performing group along with a gesture from the arms and hands is extremely effective for entrances. The eyes can also affirm that a specific signal will be delivered to the appropriate soloist or section.

Facial gestures can enhance the conducting gestures of the arms and hands, or they can remain neutral. It is even possible for them to detract from the gestural drama being acted out on the conductor's stage against the body backdrop. Be careful not to react in a negative way with your face. This distraction can preoccupy your ensemble's attention.

Three Functions of Conducting

The body actors used to execute precision conducting convey, in a nonverbal manner, the three functions found in the discipline of gestural conducting:

1. Meter/Tempo
2. Interpretive
3. Start/Entrance—Stop/Cutoff

Each function is critically important for communicating precise conducting gestures to players and singers, and defines the role of the arms, the principal actors on the conductor's stage, as well as the hands and other body actors.

While the stereotype—even the cartoon image—of the conductor has his or her arms flapping in conducting patterns (the Meter/Tempo function), the true artist-conductor emerges as a result of exceptional gifts in the Interpretive function of conducting.

The Meter/Tempo Function—An Overview

By definition, music is sound organized in time. Although the organization of music has changed over the centuries, it has always relied on the meter and tempo inherent in all music.

Early music was metered by note values as they related to rhythmic modes. Common practice and oral tradition, as well as verbal indications in the score, determined tempo as did theoretical treatises, which chronicled performance practices through the ages.

By the seventeenth and eighteenth centuries, meter and tempo indications were clearly written in the musical score. This practice of organizing the musical score with measures and bar lines continued through the Classical and Romantic periods and much of the twentieth century.

Traditionally, meters are straightforward and can be categorized as either duple (twos) or triple (threes) and simple or compound (which are derived from simple meters by multiplying them by 3). The tempo and meter designations also commonly apply to large sections, even movements, of a work. It is, however, the nature of composition to use meter and tempo to add variety, so changes are always possible at any moment and should always be anticipated. Furthermore, Twentieth-century music has brought us irregular meters as well as the frequent mixing of meters (called *multimeter*).

Specific meter classifications are outlined below:

1. Duple Meters—Groups of two and multiples of two.
   a. Simple— $\frac{2}{2}, \frac{2}{4}^*, \frac{2}{8}$
   b. Compound— $\frac{6}{2}, \frac{6}{4}, \frac{6}{8}^*$
2. Triple Meters—Groups of three and multiples of three.
   a. Simple— $\frac{3}{2}, \frac{3}{4}^*, \frac{3}{8}$
   b. Compound— $\frac{9}{4}, \frac{9}{8}^*$
3. Quadruple Meters—Groups of four and multiples of four (which are sometimes included with duple meters).
   a. Simple— $\frac{4}{2}, \frac{4}{4}^*, \frac{4}{8}$
   b. Compound— $\frac{12}{2}, \frac{12}{4}^*, \frac{12}{16}$
4. Irregular Meters—Those not evenly divisible into groups of 2s or 3s. Examples include $\frac{5}{4}^*, \frac{5}{8}, \frac{7}{4},$ and $\frac{7}{8}^*$. These meters are normally treated as some combination of 2s and 3s. For example $\frac{5}{4} = \frac{2}{4} + \frac{3}{4}$ or $\frac{3}{4} + \frac{2}{4}; \frac{7}{8} = \frac{3}{8} + \frac{2}{8} + \frac{2}{8}$ or $\frac{2}{8} + \frac{2}{8} + \frac{3}{8}$, etc.

   * These are some of the more common meters and are addressed specifically in Part Two.

Other elements that impact the Meter/Tempo function are those that suspend time in a composition, including the *fermata* (or hold), *tenuto* and *allargando*. Although the handling of these elements is an interpretive matter, accomplishing them technically is considered part of the Meter/Tempo function.

Right and Left Arms

Tradition asserts that the right arm is used to signal the Meter/Tempo function, leaving the left arm for the Interpretive functions, including phrasing, dynamics, dynamic shadings, and sustaining gestures.

This is not to suggest that the arms function separately from one another. Rather, the conductor must develop the ability to coordinate all of the functions of conducting between arms, hands, fingers, head, face, and body. Furthermore, every aspect of the Interpretive function must exist within the gestures used in the Meter/Tempo function. For example, a four-beat pattern is conducted within the framework of *staccato*, *legato*, etc; dynamic shadings are indicated in the size of the Meter/Tempo gesture, as well as through the gestures of the non-meter/tempo arm.

The Interpretive Function—An Overview

Music is an audible expression of a composer's emotions and thoughts organized into musical sounds. While these organized sounds are incapable of conveying concrete meaning, they are nevertheless expressive. It is the task of the conductor to accurately interpret and convey to an audience the musical intentions of the composer to the best of his or her ability. This calls on the conductor to attempt to enter the mind of the composer, the spirit of the text, or the message of the music.

Accomplishing this task encompasses every aspect of the musical score: meter, tempo, dynamics, phrasing, character, and so on. It includes everything from solo lines to full-ensemble passages. Every dimension of the score is under the scrutiny and interpretation of the conductor. And while the challenge of meter and tempo is no small task, it is not nearly the challenge that the emotional elements of dynamics, phrasing and other interpretive characteristics present.

The indications given in the musical score provide some assistance to the conductor, but not only are they absent at times, there is a great deal in the music that is not indicated. Therefore, it is the task of the conductor to interpret the information that is available and put it towards an accurate performance. This is an enormous task and leadership responsibility.

The Interpretive function includes a long list of musical considerations, as illustrated by this list of just some of the interpretive challenges placed upon the conductor: *forte*, *piano*, *mezzo piano*, *accelerando*, *sforzando*, *ritardando*, *legato*, *marcato*, *staccato*, and *tenuto*. Notice that Meter/Tempo terms such as *accelerando* and

ritardando are included, as they are subject to the Interpretive function of conducting as well. Also, terms such as *fuoco*, *passione* and *giocoso* call upon a conductor's interpretive skills.

The left arm is responsible for the Interpretive function of conducting. However, the right arm, face, hands and all of the gestural tools of conducting help reflect the interpretive character of music. Even the Meter/Tempo function operates with sensitivity toward the interpretation of the musical score.

In general, the Interpretive function is conveyed through degrees of *legato* and non-*legato* gestures— *molto legato*, *legato*, *marcato*, *accented*, *staccato* (to name a few). These are designated by horizontal and vertical lines organized by circles, arcs, angles, and stops, and set apart by the unique characteristics of a conductor's individual style.

The Start/Entrance—Stop/Cutoff Function— An Overview

Starting and stopping a piece of music can be taken for granted by some, but no conductor can afford to take this function lightly. It is a short moment, to be sure, but it is a critical moment. While music notation seems to clearly designate issues such as entrances and exits, there is still room for disagreement. The performing forces depend upon the conductor for precise entrances and cutoffs, and it is the role of the conductor to provide such clarity for the ensemble.

The cue for starting a musical work may seem as simple as lifting the hand or baton. However, the preparation gesture must firmly establish interpretive elements such as meter and tempo, and the character of the very first note. These issues must be firmly settled in the mind of the conductor before the first beat's preparation is signaled.

A similar responsibility is that of starting individual soloists and sections of musicians through cueing. Even virtuoso musicians depend on the conductor to confirm entrances because it helps to guarantee a precise and inspired performance.

Stopping a musical work may seem as easy as ceasing all conducting gestures, but unless the desired concluding moment is clearly gestured to all performers, a precise cutoff will not be accomplished. The same is true for any internal stops.

The hands are the most precise tool for the Start/ Entrance and Stop/Cutoff function, but it can be signaled by any of the gestural tools at the command of the conductor. In particular, facial features can be great reinforcement and should be used intentionally to strengthen these gestures.

Preparing the Conducting Technique

The process of preparing all of these areas prior to the rehearsal and performance requires a level of discipline similar to internalizing the score. But now, in addition to the mental skills developed in the analysis and internalization process, we add motor skills.

The physical activity of conducting is a motor activity that requires the coordinated engagement of head, arms, hands, and body. The final discipline in the preparation process involves preparing and practicing actual cues and gestures.

Part Two: The Meter/Tempo Function

The gestures for meter and tempo are forever interrelated. Not only does tempo proceed through the pace of the meter gesture, the tempo affects the conductor's ability to manipulate the perception of weight in the arm and the flow of the arm from beat to beat. Consequently, it is the tempo and meter, in combination, which determine the conducting pattern.

A rapid tempo will negate the attempt to use multiple dramatic pulses in a measure, while a slow tempo may demand the subdivision of pulses within a measure. For example, a fast tempo in triple meter may necessitate a one pattern rather than a three pattern. A slow tempo in duple meter may necessitate a subdivided two or four pattern. A fast tempo in an irregular meter of fives or sevens may necessitate an asymmetric two or three pattern, while a slow tempo may call for one pulse per beat.

Another factor in the choice of meter gesture is the importance of different pulses within the measure or phrase. A *hemiola* (or "two-against-three") passage may render the chosen pattern obsolete, even counterproductive. A series of accented beats that fall on the weak beats of a pattern necessitates the modification of the pattern. Many examples in the literature—especially those from the Renaissance, the late nineteenth century (Romantic), and the Twentieth century—do not conform to generic meter patterns of two, three and four. In fact, traditional patterns can injure some literature from those periods.

A balance of the Meter/Tempo function with the Interpretive and Start/Entrance and Stop/Cutoff functions must always be maintained. While meter must always be clearly conveyed to the performers, it should not override the interpretive demands of the score. When meter is the only concern, the conductor is indeed reduced to a metronome and the performance may be stifled. On the other hand, when the performers do not understand meter, the organization of the performance may suffer, rendering the conductor obsolete.

Preparation, Delivery and Rebound

Before describing the various duple, triple and quadruple meter gestures, the three elements of a beat gesture—preparation, beat/point of beat and rebound—must be analyzed and understood.

1. Preparation

This element signals every musical intention of the conductor, and it is the successful execution of the preparation that determines his or her ability to affect the sound of the performers. It also signals every aspect of the character of the intended sound: the meter, tempo, dynamic level, and all other matters of interpretation.

The gesture of preparation is determined by the initial note values of a composition. There are three possibilities:

1. If the opening note value is equal to one or more pulses, then a full preparation, beat, and rebound gesture are used.

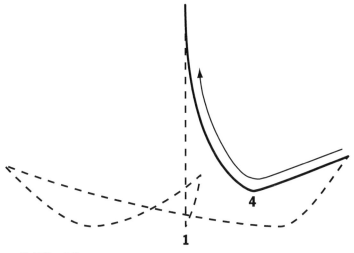

Full-Beat Prep

2. If the opening note value is equal to one-half the value of the first pulse, then the point-of-beat gesture only for the pulse immediately preceding the entering sound is used.

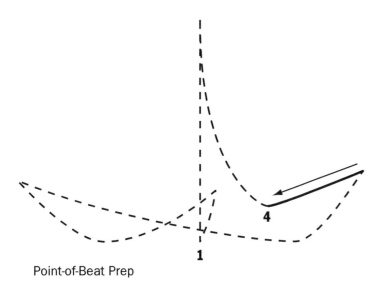

Point-of-Beat Prep

3. If the opening note value is less than one-half the value of the first pulse, then the beat and rebound gesture for the preceding beat is used.

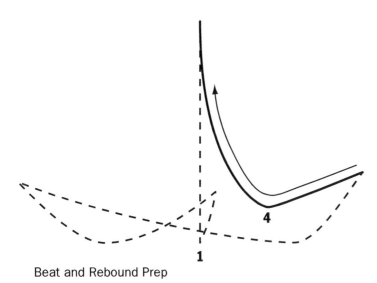

Beat and Rebound Prep

After the initial gesture of preparation, the beat and rebound function together as the gesture of preparation for the sounds that are to follow. Stops and starts in the flow of the music will necessitate additional gestures of preparation throughout a score.

2. Beat/Point of Beat

The beat is divided into the ceiling and floor of the beat gesture. The motion from ceiling to floor is the beat gesture. The point of beat occurs at the moment when the beat gesture, moving downward from the ceiling of the pattern, makes contact with the conducting floor. This point is traditionally termed the *ictus*. This element participates in the character of the sound desired, but serves specifically to maintain the cueing function, as it is the beat that definitively marks where the desired sound is to occur in time.

As explored in Part One of this chapter, the trunk of the body provides a backdrop for the vertical beat. Just as centering the pattern within that backdrop allows the strongest statement, it is the floor of the beat gesture that is the most dramatic point of contact. The point of beat should be made at the center of the body backdrop and at the floor of the conducting plane for maximum effectiveness.

Conversely, if a conductor wishes to weaken any statement he or she can move it to the far left, far right, or above the body. Similar logic follows for beat gestures, which can be weakened by raising the conducting floor—the higher the floor, the weaker the dramatic effect. This again is similar to actors on a theatrical stage delivering the lines and actions off stage.

3. Rebound

The rebound is an immediate reaction to the point of beat. In all instances, except for the downbeat, the rebound occurs at approximately a 90-degree angle upward from the slant of the preceding beat. (The rebound for the downbeat varies in relationship to the meter.) The rebound becomes the principle gesture in the preparation of the next sound to come. Once the sound has started, the only gestures that can indicate a desired change in the character of sound are the rebound and the beat that follows.

In other words, the rebound serves as the preparation for the next sound to come. Most of the time, the rebound gesture will proceed in the same style as the previous preparation and beat. However, when characteristics change from beat to beat it is the rebound that prepares the change.

Conducting Patterns

The basic conducting patterns are Two, Three, Four, Subdivided Three and Four, Six, and One. While directly related to the metrical groups discussed in Chapter 6, conducting patterns are more practical, if you will, and concern themselves with the strong musical pulses of a measure. For example, there are times when music in a compound duple meter like ⁶₈ will have 6 strong pulses (and therefore require the six pattern), but in a fast tempo, ⁶₈ will likely have only 2 strong pulses (dictating a two pattern). These basic patterns can accommodate the various simple and compound meters and each is presented and illustrated below. Irregular meters are achieved with modifications to several of the basic patterns and are also explained and illustrated.

It is important to practice these patterns until the motion is fluid and comfortable. One helpful exercise to aid in this study is to photocopy and enlarge each pattern so it is large enough to trace as an actual conducting pattern. For more realistic practice, conduct these patterns againt a recording in the meter you are practicing.[8]

The Two Pattern

When a measure or phrase is organized with one strong downbeat or principal accent per measure and only one other strong pulse in the measure, as is the case in $\frac{2}{2}$ or $\frac{2}{4}$, a two-pattern gesture should be used. A two-pattern gesture would also be used if the meter called for five or six divisions of time per measure, but only two principle pulses (e.g., a fast $\frac{5}{8}$ or a fast $\frac{6}{8}$ meter).

In the two pattern, the downbeat or first beat of the gesture begins at the ceiling and direct center of the conducting stage and descends vertically to the stage floor where the first beat's actual point of beat occurs. The rebound for the downbeat proceeds up and to the right of the conductor at a 45-degree angle. *The palm of the hand always faces the next point of beat.* The rebound stops at the halfway point in the right side of the conducting stage.

The second beat of the gesture proceeds to the middle of the conducting stage at the midpoint of the conducting backdrop. The point of beat of the second beat occurs near the vertical line of the downbeat at the center of the body. This pulse is perceived as weaker than beat one because its point of beat occurs off the conducting stage floor. (A conductor can achieve an even weaker beat two by moving the point of beat to the right or left of the vertical centerline. This gesture minimizes the use of the body backdrop thereby weakening the perception of the pulse.) The rebound for beat two is a direct line from the point of beat two, back to the ceiling for a repeat of beat one.

A two pattern is generally used when a $\frac{6}{8}$ meter is indicated in a tempo faster than 60 beats per minute. When a musical score calls for a fast $\frac{6}{8}$ meter (i.e. dotted quarter = 60 beats per minute), a two pattern is generally used. This pattern is identical to the duple two-beat pattern. However, since a fast $\frac{6}{8}$ generally calls for a strong pulse on beats one and four (out of six), a strong second beat is generally used. This stronger beat occurs in the two pattern by adding a perception of strength or weight in the preparation, point of beat, and rebound for the second pulse of the measure.

---

[8] Appendix D includes a list of recommended titles and recordings for each pattern/meter.

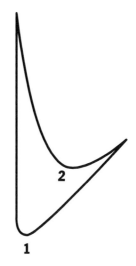

Two Pattern ($\frac{2}{4}$)

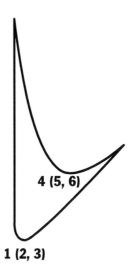

Two Pattern ($\frac{6}{8}$)

The Three Pattern

When the measure or phrase indicates an organization of a strong downbeat (or one principle accent per measure) with two additional pulses in the measure, (e.g. $\frac{3}{4}$) a three-pattern gesture is used.

In the three pattern, the downbeat or first beat of the gesture begins at the ceiling and direct center of the conducting backdrop and descends vertically to the stage floor of the conducting arena where the actual point of beat for the first beat occurs. (This is the identical gesture described and used for all downbeats in all patterns.) The downbeat's rebound proceeds up and to the left of the conductor at a 45-degree angle. The palm of the hand always faces the next point of beat. The rebound stops at the halfway point in the left side of the conducting arena.

The second beat of the gesture proceeds to the conducting stage floor at the extreme right of the conducting arena. The point of beat two occurs on the stage floor at the extreme right of the body backdrop. This pulse is perceived as the second strongest beat of the measure, second only to the downbeat. This perception occurs as a result of the gesture sweeping across the body backdrop in a downward motion. The rebound for beat two proceeds up at a 90-degree angle to the conductor's right and is completely off of the plane of the conductor's body backdrop. Again, the palm of the hand points to the next point of beat.

Beat three proceeds to the center of the body backdrop, halfway up the trunk. The rebound for beat three proceeds back to the starting location for the downbeat, with the palm of the hand facing down or, as always, toward the next point of beat. This beat is perceived as the weakest beat of the measure.

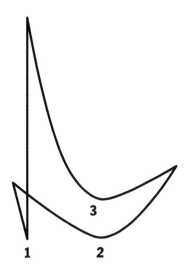

Three Pattern

The Four Pattern

When the measure or phrase indicates that the beat grouping should have a strong downbeat and three other pulses of varying strengths in the measure, (e.g. any simple or compound quadruple meters) a four-pattern gesture should be used. The four pattern uses the strong backdrop of the body to heighten the perceived weight of the pulses within the meter. The most dramatic gestures in the four pattern are beats one and three, which use the full backdrop of the trunk of the body.

The downbeat gesture, which moves from the ceiling of the conducting stage straight down the body to the floor of the stage, is the strongest motion. The next strongest motion is the slanted motion that proceeds from the conductor's left shoulder to the floor of the conducting stage on the right side of the conductor. This gesture is reserved for the second strongest musical pulse: beat three. Just as with the two pattern, the weaker beat in the four pattern will use less of the body backdrop and will have a higher stage floor for the point of beat.

The downbeat for the four-beat pattern begins in the center of the body, at the ceiling of the conducting backdrop, and proceeds to the floor for the point of beat. The rebound

for the downbeat (which serves to prepare a neutral-to-weak beat two) proceeds at a 45-degree angle halfway up the body backdrop and to the conductor's right. The palm of the hand should always face the point of beat being approached next.

Beat two proceeds across the body backdrop to the conductor's left. The point of beat for beat two is at the stage floor of the conducting arena at the furthermost left point of the body backdrop. The rebound for beat two proceeds upward at a 90-degree angle to the conductor's left shoulder, with the palm of the hand pointing to the next point of beat.

Beat three will be the second-strongest gesture, as it proceeds across the body backdrop to the floor of the conducting stage at the furthermost right point of the body backdrop. The rebound for beat three proceeds at a 90-degree angle to the conductor's right, a distance halfway up the body trunk, but outside the body backdrop. The palm faces the next point of beat. This position, by earlier definition, is a weak location that is generally appropriate for the fourth beat.

Beat four proceeds to the center of the body backdrop, halfway up the trunk. The rebound for the beat-four point of beat proceeds back to the starting location for the downbeat, with the palm of the hand facing down or, once again, toward the next point of beat. The gesture for beat four, with its point of beat and rebound, is the same as that for the final beat of the two pattern, as well as that for the third beat in the three pattern. Each of these are inherently weak gestures, but may be modified by utilizing more (or less) of the body backdrop.

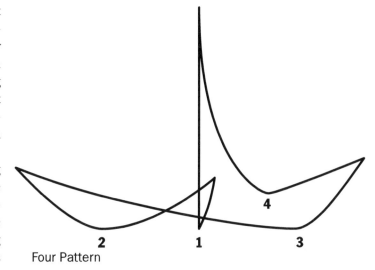

Four Pattern

The Subdivided Three and Four Patterns

Subdivided patterns are generally reserved for compound triple or quadruple meters, like $\frac{9}{8}$ or $\frac{12}{8}$, or very slow passages (quarter = 40, or slower) of $\frac{3}{4}$ or $\frac{4}{4}$ where extreme clarity is needed. Because, in these instances, there are generally only three or four strong pulses with

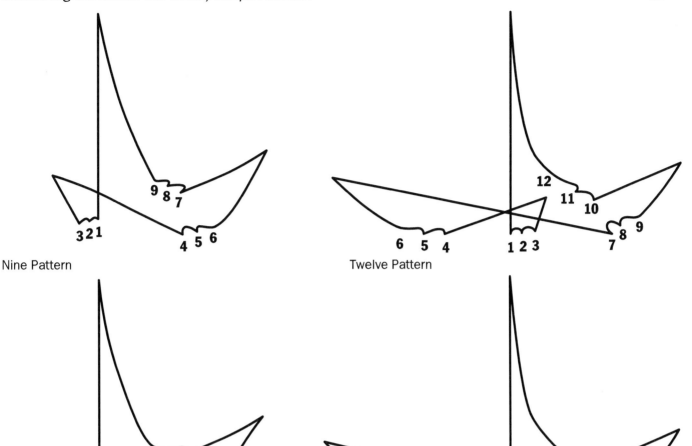

Nine Pattern

Twelve Pattern

Subdivided Three Pattern

Subdivided Four Pattern

weak subdivided pulses, variations of the three pattern or four pattern can be used.

A simple rule to ensure this emphasis on the strong pulses is to keep the primary beats as they were in the basic pattern and then add a second or a third pulse to the existing framework of each beat. These additional pulses, which are determined by the meter (a subdivided $\frac{3}{4}$ or $\frac{4}{4}$ requires a second; a slow $\frac{9}{8}$ or $\frac{12}{8}$ requires a second and third), should occur in the same direction that the primary beat was placed on the conductor's stage floor. The exception to this rule occurs on beat one, which is, by definition, a vertical beat from the ceiling of the pattern straight down to the stage floor of the conducting arena. In this instance, subdivisions should be placed in the direction opposing the next beat, which properly prepares the approach for beat two's point of beat.

To further keep the subdivided pulses weak, they should be performed with little perception of weight in the arm, hands and wrist. This will add additional emphasis to the main beats in a subdivided pattern so that clarity is maintained.

The Six Pattern

When the measure indicates an organization of two strong beats, each of which is followed by two secondary pulses (e.g. $\frac{6}{8}$), a six-beat gesture is used. In the six pattern, the downbeat or first beat of the gesture begins at the ceiling and direct center of the conducting arena and descends vertically to the stage floor of the conducting arena where the actual point of beat for the first beat occurs. (Again, this is the identical gesture for all downbeats in all patterns.)

The rebound for the downbeat proceeds slightly up and to the left of the conductor to create the two secondary beats that follow. These two minor beats bounce to the left; the palm of the hand faces down. The rebound for the third beat bounces high and to the left side of the body backdrop, exactly in the manor of the second beat in the three-beat pattern and the third beat in the four-beat pattern. The angle of this rebound is 45 degrees. The palm faces the right side of the body.

The point of beat for the fourth beat in the six-beat pattern is identical to the second beat in a three-beat pattern, or the third beat in a four-beat pattern. It is the second strongest pulse of the measure, and therefore proceeds horizontally across the body backdrop to the extreme right side of the body, with the point of beat falling on the conducting stage. The rebound of beat four proceeds up and to the right of the previous point of beat.

Beat five continues back down in the same direction, which is to the right of the conductor. The rebound of beat five is similar to the rebound of beat two in the three-beat pattern, or beat three in the four-beat pattern in that it goes out and to the right, once again at a 45-degree angle.

Beat six proceeds to the center of the body backdrop, halfway up the trunk. Its rebound proceeds back to the starting location for the downbeat, with the palm of the hand facing down. This beat is perceived as the weakest beat of the measure and is identical to all final beats of any and all beat patterns.

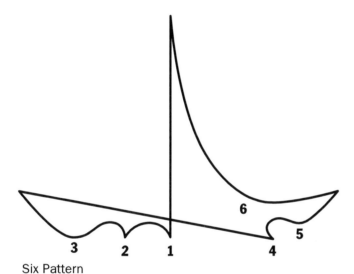

Six Pattern

The One Pattern

When the measure calls for only one strong pulse per measure, as in a fast $\frac{3}{4}$ or a fast $\frac{3}{8}$ meter, a one-beat pattern is used (quarter = 140 and above). In the one pattern, the downbeat is the only beat in the measure. The downbeat begins like all other downbeats—at the ceiling and direct center of the conducting stage—and descends vertically to the stage floor of the conducting arena where the point of beat occurs. The rebound proceeds up and to the right of the conductor in a 45-degree arc that returns to the place where the downbeat began—at the center and ceiling of the conducting stage. This quick motion resembles an archer's bow.

As the hand returns to the beginning point of the downbeat, the hand is suspended at that location for a moment before repeating the next downbeat. This suspension helps define the separate beats and keeps the pattern from becoming a perpetual circling action.

Following the rules for the gesture of preparation outlined earlier, the gesture of preparation for the one-beat pattern is a full-beat preparation, beginning from the same position at the top and center of the conducting backdrop.

One Pattern

Irregular Meters

Irregular meters (e.g. $\frac{5}{4}$, $\frac{5}{8}$, $\frac{7}{4}$, $\frac{7}{8}$) can best be thought of as asymmetrical combinations of twos and threes. For example, $\frac{5}{4}$ can be organized as 2+3 or 3+2. $\frac{7}{8}$ can be organized as 3+2+2 or 2+3+2, etc. Irregular beat patterns, which follow this same logic, are variations of two-beat (in the case $\frac{5}{4}$ and $\frac{5}{8}$) or three-beat patterns ($\frac{7}{4}$ or $\frac{7}{8}$) and may be thought of as irregular duple or irregular triple, respectively.

Irregular meters can exist in both fast and slow music and the gestures vary depending upon the tempo of the work. In slow music, where each beat will be pulsed, there is one set of patterns to consider. When the tempo prevents the pulsing of each beat, there are separate considerations. There are, however, some universal principles that drive pattern selection for both slow and fast tempos.

The most important analytical question to be asked is, "after the downbeat, what is the most important beat?" The correct gesture can be determined by the answer to this question. For example, if the two strong beats of a $\frac{5}{4}$ measure are one and three (or 2+3), the gestural pattern will follow one course. If the two strong beats are on one and four (or 3+2), the gestural pattern follows another course. The same is true for the seven-beat measure.

Five and Seven Patterns

If the second most accented beat of a $\frac{5}{4}$ measure is beat three, and tempo or stylistic concerns dictate that all beats will be pulsed, then the gesture for the third beat must go from the conductor's left shoulder across the body backdrop to the bottom right side of the con-

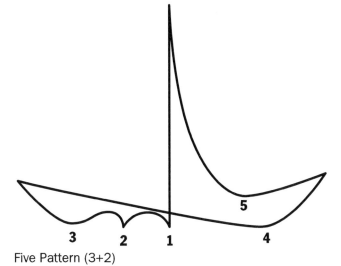

Five Pattern (3+2)

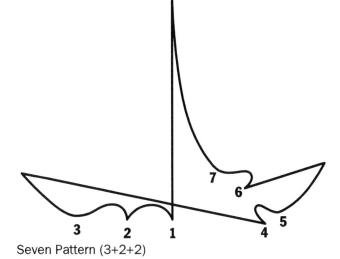

Seven Pattern (3+2+2)

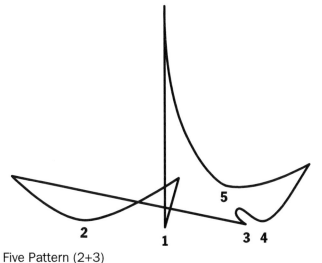

Five Pattern (2+3)

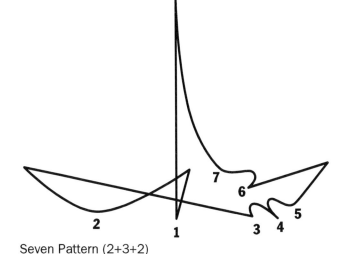

Seven Pattern (2+3+2)

ducting stage. If the third beat is the second most accented beat, then it is the third beat which must move from the conductor's left shoulder across the body backdrop to the bottom right side of the conducting stage. In both irregular duple and irregular triple, beat five is generally the weakest beat of the measure. As such it follows the same course as the final beat in any pattern.

Seven-beat patterns, or irregular triple patterns, are built within the framework of a three-beat pattern and their three strongest beats will be placed exactly within a $\frac{3}{4}$ pattern. Therefore, if beat three is a strong beat (2+3+2), the gesture for beat three should cross the body backdrop from the upper left shoulder area to the bottom right on the conducting stage. If the next strongest pulse is beat five, then this beat occurs at the same place as beat three in the three beat pattern. The principle at work here is that the pattern uses preexisting patterns for the outline, adding additional pulses within the pattern on the irregular beats. (This is similar in concept to the subdivided gestures.)

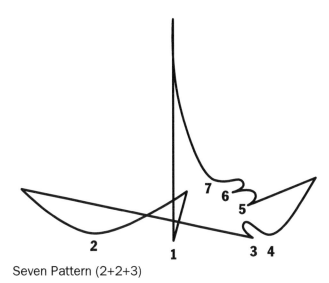

Seven Pattern (2+2+3)

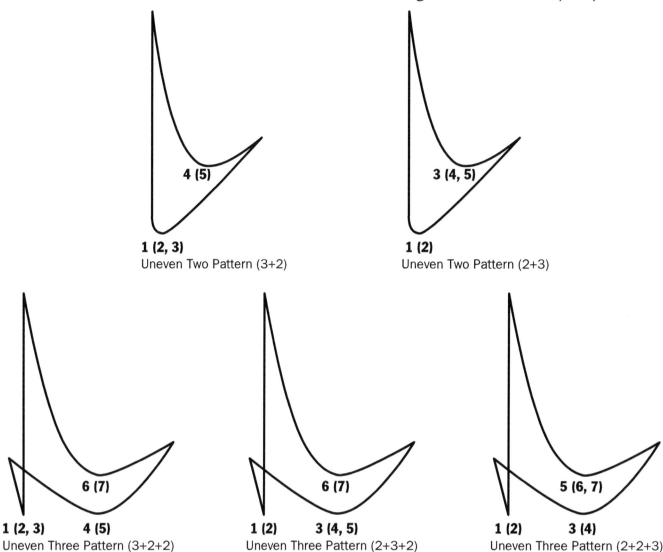

4 (5)

1 (2, 3)
Uneven Two Pattern (3+2)

3 (4, 5)

1 (2)
Uneven Two Pattern (2+3)

6 (7)

1 (2, 3)   **4 (5)**
Uneven Three Pattern (3+2+2)

6 (7)

1 (2)   **3 (4, 5)**
Uneven Three Pattern (2+3+2)

5 (6, 7)

1 (2)   **3 (4)**
Uneven Three Pattern (2+2+3)

Uneven Two and Three Patterns

When conducting music in an irregular meter at a fast tempo, the two pattern or the three pattern is used with an elongation of the beat that has the added pulse. Even more than the five and seven patterns, the uneven gestures give validity to the term irregular, and are also called *asymmetrical* patterns.

Tempo

Tempo will always effect the decision the conductor must make regarding the meter pattern to be employed, hence it must always be carefully analyzed.

We return to our earlier example: if a fast tempo is indicated for a piece of music in $\frac{6}{8}$ meter, the conducting pattern chosen will likely be a two-beat pattern. If the tempo indicated or desired is slow, the choice will likely be a six-beat pattern. Or, if the conductor determines that the $\frac{6}{8}$ piece of music is slow but very *legato* in character, the choice may be a two-beat pattern conducted almost as if the beats were *tenuto*, with the conductor giving strong pulses on both beats one and four.

Tempo in conjunction with meter will, in every instance, determine the correct conducting pattern to be used. Therefore, it is imperative that the music be analyzed in the early study stages in order to be able to determine the correct gestures for the work.

Suspension of Tempo

The suspension of tempo occurs when one encounters a *fermata*, *tenuto*, or any other pause on a held sound or rest. Of these, the most varied is the *fermata*, or hold. In general, it is indicated in the conducting pattern by creating a perception of "pulling the rebound," or a perception of weight in the arm, but its specific treatment can vary depending upon what follows the *fermata*.

1. Holds followed by a rest or cutoff

If a rest or a cutoff follows the hold, the rebound is pulled from the point of beat, and concluded with a cutoff gesture. Be certain the rebound for the cutoff gesture prepares the hand and arm for the next gesture of preparation. Motion must be completely stopped after the rebound.

2. Holds followed by another hold

If a hold is followed by another hold, the rebound of the first hold is pulled from the point of beat, then released by returning to the original tempo as the second hold is approached. Then, immediately at the point of beat, the second hold is gestured by again pulling the rebound through the pattern.

3. Holds followed by the continuation of sound in tempo

When the tempo resumes immediately after a hold, the hold is initially treated as outlined above. When the desired length of the hold is completed, the beat pattern continues in tempo, moving smoothly into the next beat. There is no breath taken by the performers after the *fermata* in a hold of this type.

Other suspensions of tempo include *tenuto*, grand pause, *fermata* over a rest, *molto ritard* or *molto allargando*, and a *fermata* over a bar line. Their treatment is similar to the pulling of the rebound described above and will be examined in more depth in Part Three of this chapter.

Terms to Memorize

The following is a list of common tempo markings. Each of the patterns outlined in this chapter should be practiced at each tempo, and all must be memorized for regular use.

Tempo and Metronome Markings

Grave (40-50)	Slow and solemn
Largo (40-60)	Very slow and broad
Lento (50-60)	Slowly
Larghetto (60-70)	Slightly faster than *largo*
Adagio (55-65)	Slowly, with expression
Andante (70-84)	Slowly, but with motion; literally "walking"
Andantino (84-100)	Diminutive; slightly faster than *andante*
Moderato (90-100)	At a moderate pace
Allegretto (100-120)	Slightly slower than *allegro*
Allegro (126-150)	Fast, lively
Vivace (140-160)	Brisk, animated
Presto (156-180)	Very fast
Prestissimo (180-208)	As fast as possible

Changes in Tempo

Accelerando (**accel.**)	Gradually faster
Allargando (**allarg.**)	Broadening
Meno mosso	Less motion, slower (*meno* = less; *mosso* = moved, animated)
Più mosso	More motion, faster (*più* = more)
Più allegro	Faster
Stringendo	Hurrying; literally "squeezing"
Rallentando (**rall.**)	Gradually slower
Ritardando (**rit.**)	Slackening
Ritenuto	Holding back

Adjustments to Tempo Interpretation

A tempo	In time; return to the original tempo marking
Ad libitum (**ad lib.**)	Freely
Fermata	Pause
Rubato	Disregarding of strict time; "stolen time," what is taken from one note is given to another later
Tenuto	Hold a note to its full value, sometimes even longer

Guide for Determining Actual Tempo

When selecting a tempo for the music, the metronome mark (MM, or beats per minute) suggested by the composer or editor should be studied and taken into account as the conductor prepares the entrance. It can also be helpful to find the tempo that is actually occurring during the process of the piece. For this, we have Cecil Effinger's system:[9]

1. Start a stopwatch on a downbeat.
2. Stop the watch on the seventh beat.
3. Compare the time on the stopwatch to the following table to find the actual metronome mark or number of beats per minute.

Seconds	MM		Seconds	MM
9	40		3.4615	104
8.57	42		3.33	108
7.82	46		3.21	112
7.2	50		3.1	116
9.9	52		3	120
2.2	60		2.85	126
5.45	66		2.7	132
5.217	69		2.6	138
5	72		2.5	144
4.736	76		2.36	152
4.5	80		2.25	160
4.285	84		2.14	168
4.09	88		2.04	176
3.913	92		1.95	184
3.75	96		1.87	192
3.6	100		1.8	200

---

[9] This system is incorporated in Mr. Effinger's Tempowatch product. Visit www.tempowatch.com for more information.

Exercises

1. Conduct all patterns with the weight of the arm focused in the fingers, rebounding off a firm surface at the point of beat. Practice all patterns at various speeds, especially working the slower tempos. Practice all patterns, beginning with different beats and thus varying the beat of preparation.

2. Conduct all patterns in each of the following manners: one measure with the right hand, then one measure with the left hand, then one measure with both hands in mirror image.

3. Practice giving the upbeat to the following pulses within a ¾ pattern, then use the same sub-pulses in a two and three pattern:
   a. - - - -
   b. -- -- -- --
   c. --- --- --- ---

4. With one beat of preparation, have a group respond by voicing the…
   a. First beat
   b. Second beat
   c. Third beat
   d. Fourth beat
   of each of the examples in exercise 3.

5. Conduct a beat pattern with the left hand, while conducting the subdivision of the pattern with the right hand. Reverse the process.

6. Repeat exercise three using slightly graduating tempi.

7. Find musical scores which include examples of all meters and practice every pattern. (Strophic hymns, carols and folk songs are a good place to begin.)

8. Using both musical scores and recordings, find examples of all meters, along with examples of multimeter (numerous changes of meter in quick succession), and practice every pattern.[10]

Part Three: The Interpretive Function

When considering the gesture used to cue the variety of interpretive beat characteristics possible in music, the foremost consideration should be what best visually exemplifies the attack and subsequent duration of the intended sound, along with the correct dynamic level. Gesture characteristics operate within a spectrum of dynamic levels that range from *pianissimo* (very soft) to *fortissimo* (very loud). Interpretive characteristics run the gamut from *tenuto* and *molto legato* (very slow and sustained) through a variety of intensities of *legato* (connected and flowing), to the extreme opposite spectrum, which includes *marcato, staccato* and the light *staccato* (detached). The level of dynamic and interpretive intensity in the arm and hand varies with each degree of change.

The interpretive gesture used for each of these musical characteristics becomes a dramatic actor imitating the intended musical sound on the conductor's stage. The conductor's challenge is to show in the most vivid and economical terms what the intended sound would look like if the arms, hands, head, and face could act it out. Each area of the conductor's gestural anatomy could be used for this imitation, but the arms are by far the most efficient and effective.

The Basic Interpretive Function

Both the right and left hands and arms of the conductor are employed to act out the Interpretive function of conducting. The consistent and principle role of the right arm is to signal meter and tempo. The Meter/Tempo function also echoes the dynamic level intended for the music. In other words, if the score calls for a *forte* dynamic level, the conducting pattern must mirror this dynamic requirement. If the score calls for a *piano* dynamic level, again the conducting pattern must demonstrate a quiet interpretation.

In addition to mirroring the dynamic level, the right arm must incorporate the interpretive characteristics, such as *legato, marcato, staccato,* etc., into its existing Meter/Tempo function. The left hand and arm are free to participate in the Interpretive function of conducting without conveying the Meter/Tempo function.

The following description of the Interpretive functions will apply both to the right and left hands and arms. Following that description, the left hand and arm will be considered separately since *crescendo* and *decrescendo*, phrasing, loud and soft, and sudden changes of dynamics as well as other possible Interpretive functions are assigned specific left-hand gestures.

Interpreting Loud and Soft Through Meter/Tempo

The Meter/Tempo function as indicated by the conducting patterns takes place within a dynamic environment. The right hand and arm must indicate the meter and tempo, and the size of the conducting pattern must mirror the dynamic level.

---

[10] A list to help you get started is included in Appendix D.

Accepting *mezzo forte* (***mf***) as the center point for the dynamic range, we can consider a basic beat pattern that fills the conducting stage and body backdrop to be reflective of this "center" dynamic. Using this as a relative point of beginning, a larger beat pattern will reflect a louder dynamic level, and a smaller beat pattern will reflect a quieter dynamic level. While the actual range of these levels will vary slightly from conductor to conductor, the relationship between the dynamic level and the conductor's pattern size increments must be consistent.

The dynamic level of the music must always be affirmed by the size of the beat patterns gestured in the right arm and hand. The gesture of preparation must prepare the dynamic level for the entering soloist, section or ensemble.

Interpreting the Musical Character

For each of the following interpretive characteristics, it is the gesture of preparation that first indicates the desired musical character. The Tempo/Meter gesture continues in this same character until the character changes. And once again, when the character changes, it is the gesture of preparation that is the first indication of the new character.

Legato

The *legato* gesture is the fundamental musical motion in the conductor's repertoire. Even if music were not ordered metrically and the only indication a conductor had to give was a constant metronomic pulse, the gesture of preparation, point of beat, and rebound require a motion that implies *legato*. Move your arm in any sort of motion. This motion itself resembles the connected quality we call *legato*. Therefore, the fundamental quality of music as well as the fundamental motion for a conductor is a *legato* gesture.

Legato is demonstrated in the arms and hands by the gentleness or strength at which the stage floor (for beats) and the ceiling (for rebounds) are approached. Further, a conductor more precisely demonstrates a *legato* line by the perceived weight seen in the flow of the arm from beat to beat.

To lessen a *legato* phrase, the floor of the beat is strong and the flow of the arm to that point is perceived as angular and light. To maximize the *legato* perception, the floor of the beat is weak and the flow of the arm between beats is perceived as circular and weighty. The extremes of this spectrum range from *tenuto*, where the floor of the beat is sustained, and the flow of the arm is pulled through the beat, to *staccato*, where the floor of the beat is extremely sharp, and the flow of the arm is agitated and swift. Circles and curves best demonstrate the perception of *legato*, while squares and angles best

exemplify the absence of *legato* and the perception of *staccato*.

This relationship also exists in the nature of an attack and the flow from sound to sound. The spectrum of sound moves from gentle origination to sharp articulation, and from long duration of individual sounds to condensed sounds. The circles relate to the gentle attacks and longer durations, while the angular squares are analogous to the sharp attacks and the compressed tones.

The very nature of most music will generally call for a *legato*-style pattern, which is achieved by moving the forearm (from the elbow forward) from point of beat to point of beat with the elbow itself remaining stationary. This is the center level in the *legato* spectrum, one where wrist and hand are not yet dramatically engaged. The weight perception in the flow of the forearm is hardly a factor.

Adding the perception of weight to the gesture will move the *legato* characteristic toward *molto legato*, and adding the perception of weightlessness to the gesture will move the *legato* characteristic toward *staccato*. The *legato* gesture is in between the two and is one which avoids extremes in expressiveness. The size of the *legato* gesture should stay within the basic backdrop arena of the trunk of the body.

As the *legato* gesture approaches the floor of the beat area, the point of contact should be blunted—neither sharp nor extremely curved. Both the sharp contact and the curved contact are reserved for characteristics to come. The *legato* gesture demonstrates a smooth continuity of sound, nothing more.

Molto Legato

As the intensity of the *legato* gesture increases toward *molto legato*, so must the intensity of perceived weight in the arm and hand increase. The curve at the point of beat should also become more circular. Or conversely, as the intensity of the *legato* increases, less angle and more perceived weight should be seen in the arm.

Perceived weight may be added by using the concept of layering. The addition of first the wrist and then the hand in the movement of the arm adds this first layer of perceived weight. Obviously, the wrist and hand were included in the initial movement of the forearm. The difference now is that the wrist pulls the hand into the stage floor at the point of contact. This creates a tug or pulling effect with the wrist and hand, as if the hand and arm are proceeding through a thick substance such as tar or taffy. This may even simulate slow motion in the arm; a perception that is a good way to practice the *molto legato* gesture.

The wrist and hand now create the curving, circular gesture desired at the point of beat. As the wrist and hand follow the movement of the forearm, the perception of weight is increased to the desired extent.

A second layer of perceived weight may be accomplished allowing the shoulder to enter the gesture. With this addition of movement in the upper arm, the elbow will begin to resemble the action seen in the wrist, as the elbow functions within the desired circular motion. Again, more perceived weight may be added by the amount of resistance and rebound effect achieved when the forearm follows the circular movement of the elbow. This layering effect can be taken to an extreme when the trunk of the body follows the movement of the shoulder, the forearm, the wrist, and the hand.

Tenuto/Fermata

Tenuto and *fermata* occurrences are the extremes in the *legato* range of gestural characteristics. While both are related to the Start/Entrance—Stop/Cutoff function of conducting, they also impact the Interpretive function because they stretch and suspend time.

The *tenuto*—the prolongation of the actual beat or note—represents a variation in the axiom of beat preparation. Therefore, a *tenuto* gesture begins not before, but immediately at the point of beat where the *tenuto* begins. At the point of beat, the entire arm rebounds with all the perceived weight and pull of the *molto legato* rebound. This weight terminates at the desired end of the *tenuto*.

If a second *tenuto* beat or note follows, a slight release of the weight should be perceived at the ceiling of the beat, with the next *tenuto* beat approached quickly and directly. The perceived weight and pull is then added again at the point of beat.

Light Staccato

The visual degrees of perceived weight demonstrated in the arms as a pattern flows contribute to the drama of the intended cue. This weight is not only perceived in the flow of the arms, but is also effected by the amount of arm used in the gesture. The least amount of arm use possible is accomplished by extending the forearm while using only the hand through the motion of the wrist. This motion creates the perception of a light *staccato*.

When using only the wrist and hand for the light *staccato* beat gesture, and combining this movement with weightless and immediate movements from beat to beat, a very precise light *staccato* is achieved. There are, however, a few other important considerations:

1. It is important to come to an abrupt stop at the top of every rebound, which further enhances the crispness achieved by the angles and quick movement from beat to beat.
2. As the beat size also effects the intended sound, the light *staccato* gesture should be quite small. Provided the gesture is performed correctly—with wrist-only movement on a stationary arm—this will be the natural result.
3. Although the wrist-only movement ensures a smaller conducting arena, be sure that the conducting patterns remain accurate.

Staccato

By introducing the forearm to the minimal gesture of conducting described above, the size of the beat is slightly increased. This layered addition of perceived weight and the resulting increase of distance between beat points indicate a heavier *staccato*. The *staccato* gesture—if points of beat remain sharp, rebounds remain angular, and perceived weight in the flow of the pattern is minimal—is effective for conducting a *staccato* character for all but the lightest of *staccato* interpretations. In both the light *staccato* and *staccato* gestures, the elbow should remain steady and stationary. And, in all *staccato* gestures, the rebound comes to an abrupt stop at the top of every rebound.

Marcato

The range of conducting gestures used to indicate musical characteristics are presented as the combination of 1) intensity of beat, coupled with 2) a perception of weight in the arm. This coupling of ingredients passes through a series of recognized musical characteristics. (It should be stated that the light *staccato, staccato,* and the *marcato* are not normative characteristics of musical sound throughout musical literature. Rather, these characteristics are exceptions to the norm.)

It is appropriate to discuss *marcato,* since it is a rather dramatic departure from the *staccato* gesture. The further addition of perceived weight by layering the elbow and the upper arm onto the *staccato* gesture moves the progression out of *staccato* into the *marcato* character. By moving the entire arm at the shoulder, the perception of weight is greatly increased in the gesture. And, similar to the light *staccato* and *staccato* character, the *marcato* gesture comes to a complete and abrupt stop at the top of every rebound.

Adding the perception of weight to the *staccato* gesture by layering the elbow is all that is needed to demonstrate *marcato*. This is, however, a significant addition. The conductor retains the sharp, angular approach to the stage floor of the beat and the abrupt stop at the top of every rebound. But because of the addition of the upper arm, the size of the beat once again is increased. This

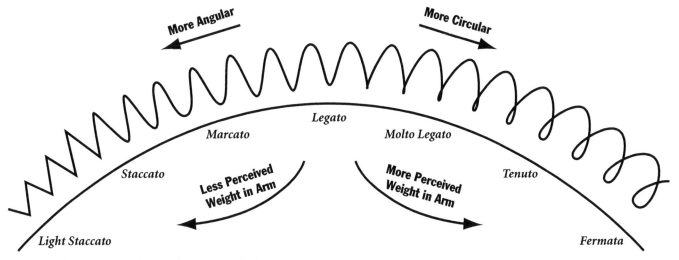

Gestural Contrasts for Musical Characteristics

layering of perceived weight and size to the pattern is precisely what cues the *marcato* character.

Accents

Conducting accents—the sudden highlight of a punctuation of sound or succession of sounds by a variety of approaches—is similar to conducting *staccato* and *marcato*. And like the *staccato* and *marcato* characters, accents are found in various dramatic intensities.

The approach to accents must emanate from the matching of accent intensity to the correct balance of beat strength and perceived weight in the arm. Furthermore, the conductor must realize that the only important gesture for achieving the desired accent is the gesture that prepares the accent due to the momentary nature of accents.

Accents are prepared by the motion of the rebound that occurs immediately before they are to sound. More specifically, they are prepared by the same gesture found in any beat of a *marcato* character. This includes the sharp, angled approach to the point of beat, but with the added perception of weight created by the use of the full arm and elbow. (The addition of a syncopated entrance or syncopation within the rhythm sometimes acts as an accent within the score. The specific gesture related to such accents is termed the gesture of syncopation and will be described in Part Four of this chapter.)

Left Hand and Arm Interpretive Gestures

The left hand and left arm have specific responsibilities related to the Interpretive function and the Start/Entrance—Stop/Cutoff function, all of which are performed free from the responsibility of meter and tempo. (While it is possible for the left hand and arm to mirror the meter gestures, this activity is often needlessly redundant and should rarely be used. One exception occurs when the music calls for extreme changes and both hands are used to forewarn an eminent change.)

The following left-hand gestures are only a few of the most commonly required interpretive gestures. Conductors should develop their own effective interpretive gestures in addition to mastering the following suggestions.

Crescendo/Decrescendo

When gesturing the *crescendo* with the left hand and arm, the palm of the hand should be placed up (cupped), and the arm should lift from the elbow to the desired level of *crescendo,* raising the arm and hand vertically. Similarly, for a *decrescendo* the cupped palm is turned gently downward and descends back to the level of the conducting stage.

These gestures are similar to lifting up and pushing down a vertical lever with the left hand and arm. Often, a *decrescendo* will follow a *crescendo,* so both characteristics should be practiced in relationship to each other.

Phrasing

A gesture that indicates the linking of notes into a phrase can be indicated in a manner similar to the *crescendo/decrescendo* gesture, except rather than a vertical movement, the gesture moves horizontally. For a phrasing gesture, the left hand begins at a position in the center of the body, and moves to the conductor's left in an upward then downward arching line, imitating the direction of the phrase (c.g., a rainbow shape). As the phrase tapers, so does the horizontal line that is moving from center to left.

A second gesture of phrasing, which indicates the tying of a note or the carrying of a breath from note to note, is a short gesture that imitates a semicircle. This tying gesture begins in the center of the body backdrop and arches up and out, descending to the center of the conducting stage.

Loud/Soft

The palm of the left hand indicates loud and soft. A palm facing up signals a loud attack or phrase, and a palm facing out toward the ensemble and slightly down signals a soft attack or phrase.

The position of the palm is also extremely influential in shaping a loud or soft attack or phrase. The palm facing out toward an ensemble is a very powerful gesture and when used, care should be taken to gently change the position of the palm. It may be helpful to think of a "gentle palm" or a "hard palm" when approaching dynamic controls with the left hand.

Suddenly Loud (*sf*)/Suddenly Soft (*sp*)

A sudden loudness of attack or a loud phrase can be achieved with an urgent, upward-facing left palm. Similarly, the positioning of the palm so that it suddenly faces the ensemble will achieve a sudden softness. In fact, if the conductor is not careful, this latter gesture could bring the sound to a complete halt.

Suspensions of Tempo

While primarily a Meter/Tempo fuction performed by the right hand, the left hand and arm can play a role in the interpretive aspect of the gesture. By extending the left hand and arm out to the performers, with the palm facing up, the left hand holds and preserves the tone while also emphasizing the hold.

Terms to Memorize

The following list includes commonly used interpretive terms. These should be memorized for regular use.

Dynamics

Pianississimo (***ppp***)	Very, very soft
Pianissimo (***pp***)	Very soft
Piano (***p***)	Soft
Mezzo piano (***mp***)	Moderately soft
Mezzo forte (***mf***)	Moderately loud
Forte (***f***)	Loud
Fortissimo (***ff***)	Very loud
Fortississimo (***fff***)	Extremely loud

Changes in Dynamics

Crescendo (***cresc.***)	Gradually louder
Più forte (***pf***)	Louder
Sforzando (***sfz***)	Sudden, strong accent
Diminuendo (***dim.***)	Gradually softer
Decrescendo (***decresc.***)	Gradually softer

Style

Animato	Animated
Cantabile	In singing style
Con brio	With brilliance
Dolce	Sweetly
Giocoso	Jokingly
Legato	Smoothly, connected
Leggiero	Lightly
Maestoso	Majestically
Marcato	With marked rhythm
Pesante	Heavily
Scherzando	Playfully
Sostenuto	Sustained
Staccato	Short, detached
Tenuto	Hold the note slightly

Exercises

1. While alternating meter gestures in the right hand, use the left hand to indicate:
   a. Four measures of *crescendo*, followed by four measures of *decrescendo*
   b. A two-measure phrase followed by a four-measure phrase
   c. Two notes that are tied together in a phrase
   d. Sudden accents, dynamic changes and changes of characteristics on varying beats
   e. Suddenly loud and suddenly soft
2. Practice all conducting meter gestures using *legato*, *molto legato*, *tenuto*, light *staccato*, *staccato*, accents, and *marcato* beat characteristics.
3. Practice all conducting meter gestures moving from *legato*, to *molto legato*, to *tenuto*, to light *staccato*, to *staccato*, to *marcato*, continually changing the character of the beat pattern with each new phrase or section of the music.
4. Practice preparing accents for various beats of various meter patterns.
5. Practice a variety of *tenuto* and *fermati* on various beats in all meter gestures and in various pattern characteristics (*legato*, *staccato*, etc.).

Part Four: The Start/Entrance—Stop/Cutoff Function

Start/Entrance Gestures

The initial downbeat of a piece of music is the most important gesture in conducting. It must signal every aspect of the character of the music. This includes both the meter and tempo of the piece, as well as the characteristics of interpretation, including dynamic level, characteristic of the beat (*staccato, legato, marcato,* etc.), and possible accents. Furthermore, the entrance gesture may signal a cue to a soloist, section or entire ensemble.

This gesture is usually given by the right arm/hand turned toward the ensemble, section or soloist. The left hand may be incorporated into the start to signal the musical character of the entrance as well. For example, a left-hand palm facing the ensemble signals a quiet entrance. A cupped palm, facing up signals a more forceful and louder entrance. The left hand may also work in cooperation with the right-hand Meter/Tempo gesture. In this case, the gesture is an outstretched arm and hand, palm up, pointed in the direction of the entering soloist, section, or ensemble; it should resemble a welcoming gesture to the performers. And again, the right and left hand may be used in combination to cue an entrance using both gestures simultaneously.

Given the importance of the Start/Entrance gesture, it must be carefully thought through at the analysis stage. This analysis must include an understanding of the Meter/Tempo intended for the beginning of a work, as well as an understanding of all aspects of interpretation to be indicated in the gesture of preparation.

Preparing Entrances

When preparing the Meter/Tempo gesture for either the initial entrance or an internal entrance, the conductor must first determine on which beat of the measure the entrance occurs.

1. Entrances on a full beat

When the entrance of a piece occurs on a note value of a full beat, the preparation for the entrance will always call for a full-beat preparation before the beat of entrance. In other words, if the entrance comes on the first beat of a $\frac{4}{4}$ measure, the preparation is the beat, point of beat and rebound of beat four in a $\frac{4}{4}$ pattern. Similarly, in a $\frac{3}{4}$ meter that has an entrance on beat two, the beat of preparation is a full beat one in the three-beat pattern.

2. Entrances on the half beat

When an entrance occurs on a note value that is exactly one half of the basic pulse of a measure (for example, the second half of beat one in a $\frac{4}{4}$ measure), the preparation is reduced to the beat in which the half beat occurs.

For example, if the music begins on the second half of beat one in a $\frac{4}{4}$ measure, the preparation beat is only the downbeat gesture for beat one with no beat of preparation. This beat begins at the ceiling and in the center of the body backdrop, and proceeds to the point of beat for beat one of the $\frac{4}{4}$ pattern. Or, if the entrance occurs on the second half of beat two in a $\frac{3}{4}$ pattern, the preparation is beat two only.

To repeat, in this type entrance the beat gesture of the beat in which the entrance occurs is the only preparation.

Gesture of Syncopation

Placing an unexpected accent on a normally weak beat produces syncopation. Tying across a strong beat or placing an accent on a weak beat can create syncopation, but the placement of a rest on the strong beat is the syncopation that most often effects entrances. These notes, which are often exactly one half of the basic pulse of a measure, are often intended to be accented. Such notes call for the gesture of syncopation, which is made exactly as described above under entrances on the half beat. The only difference is that this gesture is made with more force (similar to the *marcato* gesture) so that it prompts the accent.

3. Entrances on less than a half beat

When an entrance occurs on a note value that is less than half the value of the basic beat of the meter, the preparation is identical to an entrance that occurs on a full beat. For example, in a moderate $\frac{4}{4}$ pattern if the entrance note is a sixteenth note, then the entrance is treated as if the entrance is on the downbeat of the measure. The theory at work here is that the full beat of preparation signals enough information to determine the length of the note of entrance.[11]

Preparing Internal Entrances

In addition to the initial entrances at the start of a work, many internal entrances occur throughout a work. Treated in a manner similar to the Start/Entrance, the cue for an internal entrance is given by the left arm and hand, which extends in a welcoming gesture to the entering soloists, section, or ensemble. The face and eyes are very effective in echoing visually what the hands are signaling and should always affirm what the entrance gesture is attempting to communicate. To the contrary, if the face and eyes do not affirm the arm and hand gestures, the intended entrance gesture is weakened. (The faces and eyes alone can also give an effective cue.)

---

[11] See illustrations on pages 37-38.

All of these internal entrance cues must be prepared at least two full beats before the entrance occurs. Whether using the right or left hand, it must be in place, prepared to give the cue, two full beats before it is needed (or four beats before the internal entrance).

Stop/Cutoff Gestures

The gesture for the conclusion of a phrase or a piece of music is divided into two types: internal stops, which include weaker phrase endings, and final stops, which signal major conclusions like the end of a movement or entire work.

Internal Stops

Internal stops are gestured with either the right hand or left hand by gently tapping the point where the cutoff, phrase ending, or stop of any kind occurs. If the stop occurs on the beat, the tap may be placed by the left hand at the point of beat stop. If the stop occurs on the half beat, the beat may be subdivided, with the tap placed on the subdivided beat point. This cutoff gesture must be prepared and ready to be used two full beats before the cutoff cue is needed.

Final stops

Gestured with either the right hand or left hand, final stops are made by strongly tapping the point of beat where the cutoff should occur. If the right hand is holding a final note, then the left hand may be the desired hand to signal the cutoff. The same is true if the left hand is holding a final note. The actual gesture for the cutoff may be a strong tap on the beat or partial beat, a tap placed by one hand into the palm of the other hand, or a full-circle motion which visually ties a knot in the space in front of the body backdrop. This final cutoff gesture must be prepared and ready to be used two full beats before the cutoff cue is needed.

The gesture for the cutoff should include a rebound, which visually echoes the reverberation of the final tone. The cutoff that resembles a tapping motion by either hand is a very precise stop. This cutoff is used effectively when the character of the final note is percussive, very precise, or even punctuated. The cutoff that resembles the tying of a knot is best used when the final note has a *legato* or more sustained quality. Again, the dramatic theory working here is that circles (the tied knot) are the gesture for *legato*, while angles (the tapped beat) are the gesture for non-*legato*.

As with internal stops, the face always affirms what the cutoff gesture is attempting to communicate. The eyebrows and forehead are very effective in echoing visually what the hands are signaling with a cutoff gesture. To the contrary, if the face and eyes do not affirm the arm and hand gestures, the intended cutoff gesture is weakened.

Precision Cutoffs

Cutoffs should imitate the intensity of the ending of the music. Often, a slight duration of sound and silence is desired at the end of the work. When such an ending occurs, the cutoff may fade, and an inexact gesture will suffice. When the cutoff needs to be exact and percussive, a very precise gesture is required.

Exercises

Start/Entrance—Stop/Cutoff Gesture*

1. With the right hand, conduct regular beat patterns, and with the left hand cue entrances on a different beat in each bar.
2. With the right hand, conduct regular beat patterns, and with the left hand cue cutoffs on a different beat each bar.
3. Practice entrances that occur on the beat, on note values that are one half of the basic pulse, and on note values that are less than one half of the basic pulse.
4. Set up an imaginary ensemble (orchestra and choir with possible soloists), mentally placing people in each section. Practice starting cues, entrances, and cutoffs while the right hand keeps the conducting meter pattern. Remember, each entrance cue or cutoff should be prepared two beats before the needed moment of execution.
5. Conduct a ¾ pattern and give a cue on every other beat.
6. Conduct a ⁴⁄₄ pattern and give a cue on every other beat.
7. Conduct all variations and subdivisions of the patterns used in examples 5 and 6, giving a cue on every other beat.
8. Repeat exercises 5–7, giving cutoffs on every other beat.

Coordination*

1. Conduct the beat pattern in one hand while conducting the subdivision of that pattern in the other hand. Repeat the exercise switching the functions of each hand.
2. Conduct one pattern in one hand, while conducting a different pattern in the other hand.
3. Practice conducting each pattern while singing an eighth-note syncopation to each beat. *Never conduct the syncopation.*
4. Conduct various meter patterns, alternating entrances on various beats with cutoffs on various beats. Use right hand cues, left hand cues, and both hands cueing in combination.

*A mirror or video camera can be a helpful tool when practicing all of these exercises.

Chapter 7: Researching the Score

In order to choose literature that will give confidence to a developing program or ensemble , it is important to first identify the type of literature desired for study or performance. Questions to consider include:

- What is the desired musical period(s) of the program?
- Who is the composer of the music?
- What is the desired voicing?
- Is the piece a major work or smaller in scope?
- What is my long-range plan for this ensemble?
- What are my obligations to these performers?

After these questions have been considered, there is another important set of questions to answer. How do I…

- Find ideas for this program?
- Know if the edition under consideration is reliable?
- Find the best edition?
- Find a choral piece written on a particular text?
- Find a complete listing of a composer's works?
- Discover the musical intentions of the composer?
- Find out if a work is still in print?

These questions reveal what type of source needs to be consulted.

Knowing the best and most appropriate sources and having a research system to discover good sources enables the conductor to find answers for all of these important questions.[12]

Primary and Secondary Sources

Source materials used by the conductor are approached from two levels: primary sources and secondary sources. Primary sources are original documents and because they are firsthand information they are considered to be the most reliable sources of research information. When data is not original to the researcher they become secondary sources. Secondary sources represent

---

[12] Please note that the placement of this discipline last is only functional, since it goes without saying that a score must be selected before any conducting is actually necessary.

varying degrees of likeness to primary sources. They also vary in degrees of reliability due to the increased level of remoteness from the original source and the various levels of the strength of scholarship used in the editing of the secondary source.

The distinctions between primary sources and secondary sources require that we consider the following questions before beginning the search for the desired edition:

- Does the literature sought merit the study of original sources?
- If so, is it possible to view the original manuscript or a facsimile?
- If not, are scholarly secondary study editions available?
- Are reliable editions available for use in performance?

Understanding the Nature of Sources

The information we know about music comes from four principle sources:

1. Documents of record, such as programs or newspaper accounts.
2. Essays and treatises on the theory and practice of music.
3. Composer biographies or contemporary accounts.
4. The musical score itself.

Conductors and performers would seem to be working with the most important source, the actual musical score. However, all musical sources are not the same. The score in the hands of the conductor or performer is at least one step removed, if not many steps removed, from the primary source—the composer's original manuscript.

Some editions are more accurate than others. The most correct edition of a score is the one that most precisely conveys the final intentions of the composer. Friedrich Hänssler, senior editor of the publishing firm Hänssler-Verlag of Stuttgart, Germany, states that the ideal edition is one that, "seeks to accurately present the composer's last wish for the composition."

However, determining the exact intentions of the composer is not as simple as rendering an exact duplication of the original manuscript. Such a rendering would fail to convey to the modern audience matters such as the reconciliation of differences in duplicate versions of the original manuscript, differences in notational practice between the time of the original manuscript and today, and questions regarding original performance practice.

Editorial Process

Editions are only as good as the scholarship that led to their publication. The ideal that any editor is working toward is a trustworthy representation of the musical intentions of the composer. If the composer is living, the published edition has the opportunity to accurately represent the composer's musical intentions and is most often accurate. However, even under these conditions mistakes are made in the printing process. These are often corrected in a second printing, but many original printings of the incorrect score will be available and widely distributed before a publication is reprinted.

If the published score is from an earlier musical period, the editorial process is critical to an accurate publication. Editorial methods vary greatly and the importance of the editor in the process cannot be overstressed; the results are crucial. The motivation to publish historical works is to direct the attention of the musical community to worthy music. Therefore, any form of simplification that makes the music immediately accessible to the greatest number of people is desirable. But however notation may be simplified, the overriding caveat is to convey accuracy.

Therefore, the most important editorial marking is the indication that distinguishes between what is original and what has been supplied or amended by the editor. Any information provided by the editor is valid, as long as the editor demonstrates the original musical markings and explains what has happened in regard to the original. The conductor must be certain that nothing has been changed from the original without some indication in the score. The use of editorial brackets or parenthesis is the common indicator of information supplied by the editor to distinguish it from original material.

Toward Ideal Sources

The ideal for every conductor is to have scholarly scores informed by the original manuscript. The opportunity to see the exact musical markings made by the composer brings great understanding and confidence to the research, interpretation and performance process. However, original scores before the 1500s are

extremely rare. This is true of all early editions and in diminishing levels of rarity as the process of music printing progressed through the centuries. Therefore, conductors, like researchers of any music, must depend upon editions of the original manuscript for study and performance.

The Search for the Right Source

In order to begin the search for literature, the conductor should ask the following questions at the outset of every program choice:

1. What kind of literature do I want to study or program?
2. What is the best source for the literature identified?
3. What process do I follow in order to review the source identified?

In general, the term *historical edition* may be applied to any music publication that is devoted to a past repertoire. The serious investigator and/or performer is interested in investigating scholarly editions, also termed *critical editions*. Such published historical editions are based upon an editorial process that involves comparing and contrasting the composer's original manuscript or other historical editions based upon the original manuscript.

The alternative to the historical/critical edition is the performance edition. The performance edition involves an editorial process, which may—but does not necessarily—use primary or scholarly secondary sources. The performance edition often does not footnote or reference its sources, and often incorporates editorial markings designed to assist in a modern performance.

The historical or critical edition and the performance edition need not be mutually exclusive in editorial process, but the fact that they are intended for two different audiences usually determines the choices made in the editorial process. The scholar expects the historical or critical edition to indicate, through verbal description and footnotes, research relative to the understanding of the original manuscript. The performer, on the other hand, expects the performance edition to render a score that is honest to the intentions of the composer, yet easily readable in a performance setting. The performance edition does not distract the performer with possibly confusing notation alternatives and descriptions printed in the musical score.

The historical edition is found in either a collected edition that contains a composer's complete compositional output, or in an anthology that contains a variety of works of a similar genre. A facsimile in which the primary source is reproduced—with or without scholarly commentary—is considered a category of the collected edition. Collected editions, anthologies, and facsimiles are usually available in ongoing series published by musicological societies and usually found in libraries.

Performance editions exist separately as independent publications due to their practical function as a performance copy for either conductor or performer. They are published in large quantities because of the needs of the performing ensembles for which they are intended. Performance editions are usually found by searching the catalogs of music publishers, by speaking with colleagues or by contacting a reputable music store.

As stated above, historical editions are based upon primary and secondary sources. Performance editions may also be based upon primary or secondary sources, as in the case of the *Urtext edition*. Urtext is a term applied to a modern printed edition of earlier music in which the aim is to present a literal rendering of the original score without editorial additions or alterations.

Although it is greatly preferred for editors to include references to source materials, many performance editions do not indicate sources. If sources are not referenced, the performer must either take the responsibility of comparing the performance edition to critical source materials, or trust the scholarship of the editor to be true to the original intentions of the composer.

Acquiring Sources

After determining the literature type and the source desired, the final step is to acquire the edition of the musical score. In some instances, more than one source may be identified. In other instances, the desired score may not be available. When beginning the quest for the source and edition desired, it is important to note the descriptive elements regarding the composition:

1. Title of composition
2. Composer and author of text source
3. Editor
4. Setting
5. Publisher and/or distributor
6. Item number
7. Copyright date or publication date

It is the rare and privileged one who has the opportunity to view original manuscripts of early music, especially if the musical score is a classic, but it is important to know that such works are indeed available and can be viewed. As you would expect, rare and important original documents are kept under lock and key and behind glass or in environmentally protected libraries or vaults. These are typically found at the important research libraries, national libraries and national archives. However, under special conditions interested researchers can view such material.

When the viewing of the original document is difficult or impossible, it is quite possible for the researcher to refer to a photographic facsimile. Manuscripts dating from as early as medieval works are available through facsimile editions. If a facsimile is not available for the desired score, the study of a primary source is still possible through Photostats specially ordered, or through microfilm or microfiche copies. Libraries and archives that have acquired historical manuscripts often make these resources available through copy services. Such formats are relatively inexpensive to acquire and are excellent sources for study. Their availability has made scholarship possible on a much broader scale, allowing researchers to command the resources of libraries around the world.

The next step for study beyond photographed likenesses of the originals comes through scholarly historical editions. Typically, such editions describe the original sources on which the modern edition is based as well as other sources for information employed. Information regarding modern scholarly editions has been consistently chronicled through journals and other periodicals dealing with historical musicology. Information about the primary sources on which modern editions are based is best obtained from the editions themselves, but this information may need to be amplified by consulting the catalogs of printed and manuscript music in a major research library.

Indispensable reference books, dissertations and catalogs exist today for locating both historical editions and performance editions of scores. Such reference materials are available in libraries with a focus on music research.

Due to the expense involved in preparing and publishing historical editions, libraries are generally the only place historical collections are found. Performance editions, on the other hand, are affordable for individuals interested in collecting and studying specific compositions. Performance editions are published with the intention of making them available to conductors on a mass scale for performance. Libraries are less likely to shelve individual performing editions of small compositions. However, major works such as symphonies, incidental music, concertos, oratorios, operas, and cantatas are often found in libraries. The performer interested in locating performing editions of smaller works must contact publishers, rental agents or retail music suppliers directly to secure a particular composition. Only the most popular of performing editions stay in print for extended periods.

References for Finding Sources

The most thorough and accessible English-language list of historical editions is found in A. H. Heyer's *Historical Sets, Collected Editions, and Monuments of Music: A Guide to Their Contents.* The most recent edition of Heyer's monumental work includes the complete editions of the music of individual composers and the major collections of music that have been published or are in the process of publication. Each entry follows the Library of Congress format and contains the composer or compiler of the collection, the title, the place of publication, the publisher, the date of publication, the paging or number of volumes, and a brief description of illustrative material. After any special notes, a listing of the contents is given. This source can be found in most good libraries.

Three other English-language works are also very helpful for identifying historical editions:

- *Historical Musicology*, by L. B. Spiess
- The list of historical editions published in Willi Apel's *Harvard Dictionary of Music*, under the entry "Editions, historical,"
- "Editions, historical," in *The New Grove Dictionary of Music and Musicians*, edited by Stanley Sadie

The German musical encyclopedia *Die Musik in Geschichte und Gegenwart* is another standard reference for scholars seeking historical editions. Collected editions and their contents are listed in this German-language reference under the heading "Denkmaler," or "monuments."[13]

Technology is being used today for viewing printed editions through images delivered electronically and viewed on a computer screen. In this process, printed editions are scanned and transferred into digital format. Images stored digitally can be viewed on screen or printed in hard copy. This process is in full commercial use with popular performing editions and with some historical editions. This technology can be used to store a full library of scholarly and performing editions to be made available to the widest possible audience through the Internet. Laser technology allows the transference of more than eight thousand pages of information to a compact disc. When this process becomes completely economical for all users, the printing of editions as we know them may become irrelevant.

---

[13] Appendix E lists other resources for researching credible sources.

Elements Contributing to an Excellent Edition

It is entirely possible to edit an historical manuscript oneself. In fact, the best way to understand the process that contributes to an edition is to work through the various steps necessary for producing an accurate historical edition. (These steps are outlined in an exercise at the end of this chapter.)

The first step in creating your own edition is to seek out the best sources for the work to be edited. This step requires securing primary or secondary sources and assessing the accuracy and reliability of these sources; it is less difficult if there is only a single source for the desired composition.

The second step in the editorial process is to compare and take into account all versions deemed reliable for the desired work. If there are several sources for the desired composition, the editor must compare and contrast these sources, always keeping in mind that the intent is to discover, as best as one can, how carefully the source mirrors the composer's final intentions for the work.

The next step in the editorial process is to consider the notational devices used in the original work, and then make decisions how best to convey the original markings into notation that has meaning to the modern reader. For early music, this is a particularly difficult task. Even as late as the eighteenth and nineteenth centuries, notation markings conveyed meanings that are interpreted differently today. The modern editor must decide whether to keep the original marking and explain the modern difference for interpretation in footnotes, or change the marking to convey modern meaning, again noting the editorial change by way of footnotes.

The fourth step in the editorial process is to factor in the performance practice. The editor must consider how the work was intended to sound during the period in which it was written. What implications do these facts have upon a modern performing edition? Composers in earlier times often left some notation or interpretive markings off their manuscript, leaving some decisions to the performer. This meant that there was a difference between how the manuscript looked and how it actually sounded. For example, in the Baroque period composers used figured bass to indicate the harmony desired for a composition. The informed keyboard player knew to render the indicated figured bass into a correct performance. However, what does the modern editor do with such markings? This is one example of the performance practice consideration every historical editor must face.

Finally, the editor must decide who the intended audience is for the edition chosen. In other words, is the edition intended to be a performing edition, or is the final work an historical/critical edition intended for scholarly study? Or, is the final edition intended to satisfy both performance and scholarly study? The Ur-text edition attempts to convey the original composer's composition without editorial markings. Such an edition translates into modern notation all the notes and details of the original manuscript. At the other extreme is a heavily edited performance edition. Characteristics of the pragmatic performance edition are exact markings for various interpretive characteristics. Such an edition makes the work immediately available for a wide group of performers. These two extremes in types of editions do not need to be mutually exclusive. If the editor is careful to clearly indicate editorial additions and interpretations from what was in the original manuscript, an edition can be both a scholarly edition and a performance edition.

Exercise

Create Your Own Edition

Following the directions outlined below, create your own researched edition of a work for study or performance:

1. Identify the best primary source or reliable secondary source(s):
   a. If an original source is available, consult this as a primary source.
   b. If more than one original source is available (copy, revision, etc.), consult each copy and compare the sources.
   c. If reliable secondary sources are available, consult and compare all secondary sources.
2. Take into account all versions deemed reliable for the desired edition:
   a. The intent is to discover, as best as one can, how carefully the source mirrors the composer's final intentions for the work.
3. Consider the notation devices used during the period of the original work:
   a. Make editorial decisions on how best to convey these notes to a modern performer.
   b. Note changes made to the score by way of footnotes or parenthesis.
4. Consider the performance factor for the era the work was composed, and consider the issue of performance in a modern setting:
   a. How was the work intended to sound when it was originally written?
   b. How can the original intentions be conveyed to a modern performer?
   c. What did performers know to do during the era this piece was written that is not indicated in the score (and that modern performers would not necessarily know to do today)?
   d. How can such performance practices be conveyed to a modern performer?
5. Decide who is the intended audience for the edition you are creating:
   a. Is this an historical edition for study only?
   b. Is this a performing edition for ease of performance only?
   c. Is this an historical/performance edition, which shows historical editorial changes, but in the context of a practical, performable score?
6. Indicate decisions made in the final edition:
   a. Either by footnotes or parenthesis, show what decisions were made that vary from the original source.
   b. Provide a cover page that indicate editorial decisions.

Appendix A

Conducting Checklist

The following table is a checklist for the conductor's preparation. It is best used when evaluating yourself or other conductors in a class or peer setting. The checklist is also helpful in thinking through all of the considerations necessary in preparing a score for rehearsal or performance, and the preparation of the conducting technique for rehearsal and performance. The list purposefully overlaps several disciplines and skills.

The conducting checklist has been organized according to the three functions of conducting: Meter/Tempo Function, Interpretive Function, and Start/Entrance and Stop/Cutoff Function. In addition, characteristics related to leadership and teaching skill are included in this checklist.

I. Meter/Tempo Function
A. Posture
   1. Stance
   2. Arm/wrist/hand position
   3. Body language
B. Downbeat/Cueing
   1. Preparation
      a. tempo
      b. dynamics
      c. beat character
   2. Position of head, arms, hands, and beat in relation to body backdrop
   3. Right- and Left-hand position
   4. Facial gestures
   5. Eye contact
   6. Overall body language
C. Conducting Patterns
   1. Meter/Tempo decision
   2. Well-defined meter patterns (all meter patterns)
   3. Subdivided meter patterns
   4. Position of conductor to performers
   5. Point of beat in relationship to body backdrop
   6. Clarity of point of beat and rebound
D. Holds
   1. Preparation for hold
   2. Execution of hold
   3. Holds followed by a rest
   4. Holds followed by a hold
   5. Holds returning to tempo

II. Interpretive Function
A. Character of interpretive gestures *(legato, tenuto, staccato, marcato)*
B. Interpretive character of beat pattern
   1. Interpretive character of the right hand (if right hand used for Meter/Tempo Function)
   2. Interpretive character of the left hand
C. Phrase definition
   1. Phrasing
   2. Starting of new phrase
   3. Ending of phrase
D. Expressiveness (Left-hand skills)
   1. Dynamics
   2. Dynamic shadings
   3. Accents
   4. Suddenly loud/suddenly soft
   5. Ritard/accelerando
   6. Mirror conducting (to be avoided)
   7. Overall left hand skills (if right hand is used for Meter/Tempo Function)
   8. Ability to alternate hands
   9. Creative Expression

III. Start/Entrance and Stop/Cutoff Function
A. Preparation of downbeat entrance
   1. Single motion preparation
   2. Character of entrance
   3. Double preparation (to be avoided)
B. Entrance/Cutoff
   1. Preparation of entrances
   2. Characteristic of cutoffs
   3. Precision cutoffs
   4. Rebound of cutoffs (preparation for next entrance)

IV. Leadership and Teaching Skills
A. Performance skills
   1. Knowledge of styles
   2. Aural skills
   3. Knowledge of pitches and rhythms
   4. Knowledge of precise intonation
   5. Knowledge of good tone quality
   6. Knowledge of balance and blend
   7. Familiarity with specific abilities of ensemble members

8. Understanding of acoustics within the performance space
9. Technical awareness
10. Understanding of technique of ensemble

B. Knowledge of score
   1. Analysis of score
   2. Internalization of score
   3. Marking of score
   4. Marking of individual parts
   5. Researching of score
   6. Score selection

C. Personality Skills
   1. Mannerisms
   2. Confidence
   3. Sensitivity and sense of humor
   4. Patience and self-control

D. Personal Traits of the Conductor
   1. Appearance
   2. Posture
   3. Grooming
   4. Distracting mannerisms (to be avoided)

E. Purpose and vision
   1. Motivational ability
   2. Communication skills
   3. Teaching ability
   4. Rehearsal planning
   5. Balance of instruction to performance
   6. Imagination
   7. Rapport
   8. Tact
   9. Respect for musicians
   10. Self critical and acceptance of criticism

Appendix B

Single-Movement Chart Exercise

Template for Single-Movement Chart

Measures Analyzed	Analysis	Rehearsal Considerations

Summary Information (Include any information that is helpful to you at-a-glance. Suggestions include: total number of measures, opening key signature, instrumentation/voicing, text source, number of themes, tempo, and time signature.)

Hodie Christus

SSA and Piano

Traditional

Taras Nahirniak

*Play notes in bracket if not using brass.

*Play right hand if not using brass.

Single-Movement Chart Analysis
"Hodie Christus"

Measures	Analysis	Rehearsal Considerations
1-20	Introduction Quarter note = 154—quarter note remains constant. *Staccato* and slurred character. Accents determine phrasing. B-flat Major	Emphasize *staccato* vs. *legato* phrasing. Accents are to be exact. Steady pulse—quarter note = 154.
21-44	8-measure phrases/question and answer $\frac{3}{8}$ and $\frac{3}{4}$ alternation Text enters. Running eighth notes. m. 43–44—Key change to C Major	Continue to emphasize appropriate accents. Keep tempo steady (no rushing).
45-64	Continuing mixed meters. Duple vs. triple C Major More *legato* phrasing. Dynamic levels.	More *legato* phrasing. Nuance of dynamic levels.
65-76	Interlude Return to *staccato* and *legato* phrasing. Asymmetrical phrases.	Distinguish accents, *staccato* and *legato* characters of line.
77-105	New text. Voices in duets. Mixed meter. Dynamic contrasts in mid-volume levels. m. 104–105—Return to B-flat Major	Tune and balance duets. Careful attention to dynamic contrasts. m. 104–105—Tune the modulation.
106-111	Transition B-flat Major Accents, *staccato, tenuto,* and *legato* characteristics	Distinguish phrasing characteristics.
112-125	Echo pattern between voices. $\frac{3}{8}$ and $\frac{3}{4}$ meters Accents determine phrasing. Building of intensity through dynamics.	Rhythmic precision between question/ answer phrases. Carefully tune chords. Observe all accents.
126-136	1st and 2nd endings New chromatic motives. Parallel 4th in voices. Dynamic modulation and building. Accents crucial to climactic ending. Repeat goes from *ff* to *sub p*.	Contrast dynamics. Carefully tune chords. Accents must be accurate and deliberate.

136 measures / B-flat Major / SSA with 3 tumpets, 2 trombones, timpani and percussion /
traditional Latin text / ABA' / ♩ = 154 / $\frac{4}{4}, \frac{2}{4}, \frac{3}{8}, \frac{6}{8}$ / percussive

Performer's Marking Sheet

Performer's Marking Sheet
"Hodie Christus"

Measures	Part	Comment
1-20	Inst.	Observe the staccato phrasing; differentiate carefully between staccato and legato as indicated; also mark every accent and differentiate between varieties of accents; keep a steady pulse at quarter note = 154. Practice with a metronome.
21-136	All	Write a word-for-word translation throughout your part:

Hodie Christus natus est;	This day Christ is born;
Hodie Salvator apparuit.	This day the Savior has appeared.
Hodie in terra canunt Angeli.	This day on Earth the Angels sing
Laetantur Archangeli.	And the Archangels rejoice.
Hodie exsultant; justi dicentes.	This day the righteous rejoice, saying
Gloria! In excelsis Deo.	Glory to God in the highest.
Alleluia Gloria! Alleluia Deo!	Alleluia, Glory to God!

Measures	Part	Comment
21	SS	*Forte* attack on "Hodie"; deliver crisp consonants for an animated beginning to the choral lines.
24-28	SS	Draw an arrow over "est" and hold through rest in m. 28.
25	A	Mark your entrance in this measure; mark the entrance *f*.
28-32	A	Draw an arrow over "est" and hold through rest in m. 32.
32-36	SS	Think the text with the altos for a uniform cutoff on the rest in m. 36.
37-40	SSA	Mark each accent on the first word of these measures.
40-41	SSA	Note the meter transition and mark it. Remember that the eighth note remains constant.
41-44	SSA	Mark the *crescendo* from **mp** to **f**.
51	SS	Note the $\frac{7}{8}$ entrance measure (the eighth note remains constant).
58	A	Your entrance imitates the soprano entrance in m. 51.
63-65	SSA	Mark the *crescendo* in all parts.
65-66	SSA	Place the "t" of "apparuit" on the downbeat of m. 66.
65-77	Inst.	Mark this section lightly and *legato*; note the transition of feeling between sections and augment this character.

Continued on next page…

77-105	SSA	Mark this section *legato* and carry all the words through to the rest marked in the line.
85-87	SSA	Mark the *mf* entrance.
92-96	SSA	Mark the contrast of the *mp* section from the *mf* section.
96	SS	Mark a *crescendo* in the measure, continuing through m. 105.
98-105	A	Join the *crescendo* that has already begun with the SS.
104	SSA	Accent each syllable.
105	SSA	Keep the "e" of "Hodie" an open vowel (eh).
105	Inst.	Return of the opening statement in the instrumental parts. Echo the opening attention to *staccato*, *marcato*, and accents.
112-113	SSA	New vocal material with the return of the same instrumental material from the beginning. Note the accents on the initial syllable of "Hodie."
114-115	SSA	Note the meter shift from $\frac{6}{8}$ to $\frac{3}{4}$ (eighth note remains constant).
120	SSA	*Forte* entrance. This is important as a contrast to the coming *sub p*.
122	SSA	Mark the *subito p* dynamic and observe immediately on the downbeat.
123-125	SSA	*Crescendo* from *p* to *ff*, and add accents on m. 125 "Gloria!"
126	SSA	Mark the repeat barline for easy identification.
126	A	Mark the *subito p* dynamic level on the downbeat.
130-136	SSA	Mark and circle every accent.
132	SSA	Draw an arrow to the repeat barline in m. 126
134-136	SSA	Highlight the *crescendo* to the final "Deo!"
136	SSA	Stop the tone on the accent "o" of "Deo!" so that the pronunciation is "aw" and not "oh." Do not close the mouth on this vowel, but rather stop the tone with mouth open.

Appendix D

Recommendations for Meter/Tempo Exercises

Recordings

The examples in this list are meant to provide a musical backdrop for the basic conducting pattern. Fairly consistent in their conducting demands, they allow you to become comfortable with the pattern in a musical context but should not require a score.

The Two Pattern

The Creation, "The Heavens are Telling"	Franz Joseph Haydn
Holberg Suite, op. 40	Edvard Grieg

The Three Pattern

Symphony No. 2 in B major, op. 36, Movement 2	Ludwig van Beethoven
Overture to *L'Italiani in Algeri*	Giocomo Rossini

The Four Pattern

Requiem in D minor, K.626, Movement 1	W. A. Mozart
Symphony No. 6 in F major, op. 68, *Pastoral*, Movement 2	Ludwig van Beethoven

The Subdivided Three and Four Patterns

Nine Pattern

Symphony No. 1 in C minor, op. 68, Movement 1	Johannes Brahms

Twelve Pattern

"Pastoral Symphony," from *Messiah*	G. F. Handel

Subdivided Four Pattern

Suite No. 3 in D, "Air"	J. S. Bach

The Six Pattern

Carnival of the Animals, "The Swan"	Camille Saint-Saëns

The One Pattern

Concerto Grosso No. 5 in D major, Movement 3	G. F. Handel
Ancient Airs and Dances, Suite No. 1, "Gagliarda"	Ottorino Respighi

Irregular Meters

Five Pattern

Take Five	Dave Brubeck

Seven Pattern

Second Essay for Orchestra	Samuel Barber

Continued on next page...

Scores

Once you feel secure with the basic pattern, it is important to begin working with examples that include varied conducting demands, such as changes in meter, tempo and musical style. Therefore, the examples listed with each pattern may not contain that pattern throughout. While recordings are available for many of the selections listed below, it is both helpful and important that you reference the score.

The Two Pattern

"Sicut Cervus"*	G. P. da Palestrina
Mass No. 2 in G major, D.167, "Gloria" and "Credo"*	Franz Schubert
Fantasia for piano, chorus, and orchestra, *Choral Fantasy*, op. 80	Ludwig van Beethoven
Symphony No. 9 in D minor, op. 125, *Choral*, "Alla Marcia"	Ludwig van Beethoven
"Lord, Thy Help I Seek and Pray For," from *Drei Geistliche Leider**	Felix Mendelssohn
Violin Concerto in E minor, op. 64	Felix Mendelssohn
Roman Carnival Overture, op. 9	Hector Berlioz
Cello Concerto in A minor, op. 129, "Sehr lebhaft"	Robert Schumann
Variations on a Theme by Haydn, op. 56a, "Chorale"	Johannes Brahms
Academic Festival Overture, op. 80, "Allegro"	Johannes Brahms
Requiem Mass, "Libera Me"	Gabriel Fauré
Peer Gynt Suite, No. 1, op. 46, "Morgenstimmung"	Edvard Grieg
Ancient Airs and Dances, Suite No. 1, "Passo mezzo e mascherada"	Ottorino Respighi
"Dide ta Deo"*	Uzee Brown, Jr.
"Eilinahu Hanavi"*	Lee R. Kesselman

The Three Pattern

Gloria in D major, RV 589, "Et in terra pax hominibus" and "Domine fili unigenite"*	Antonio Vivaldi
Messiah, "And the Glory of the Lord"*	G. F. Handel
Symphony No. 39 in E-flat major, K.543, "Minuet"	W. A. Mozart
Mass No. 2 in G major, D.167, "Kyrie"*	Franz Schubert
Stabat Mater in F major/F minor, D.383*	Franz Schubert
Overture to *Tannhäuser*	Richard Wagner
Elijah, op. 70, "Hear Ye, Israel"	Felix Mendelssohn
L'Arlésienne Suite, No. 1, IV. "Carillon"	Georges Bizet
Variations on a Theme by Haydn, op. 56a, Variation IV	Johannes Brahms
Vier Quartette, op. 92, No. 1 "O schöne Nacht"*	Johannes Brahms
Violin Concerto in D Major, op. 35, II. "Canzonetta"	P. I. Tchaikovsky
"Fantasia on a Ukrainian Carol"*	arr. William Cutter

The Four Pattern

"Musica Dei donum optimi"*	Roland de Lassus
Gloria in D major, RV 589, "Gloria in excelsis Deo"*	Antonio Vivaldi
Cantata No. 79, *Gott der Herr ist Sonn und Schild*, "Chorus"	J. S. Bach
Messiah, "For Unto Us a Child is Born" and "Glory to God"*	G. F. Handel
"Alles hat seine Zeit"*	Franz Joseph Haydn
Te Deum in C major, K.141, "Te Deum Laudamus"*	W. A. Mozart
Piano Concerto in C minor, op. 37, "Allegro"	Ludwig van Beethoven
L'Arlésienne Suite, No. 1, Movement 1	Georges Bizet
Vier Quartette, op. 92, No. 3 "Abendlied"*	Johannes Brahms
Symphony No. 5 in F major, op. 76, B.54, Movement 2	Antonín Dvořák
Symphony No. 5, op. 64, Introduction to Movement 1	P. I. Tchaikovsky

* Scores for those selections marked with an asterisk are included in the *Precision Conducting Anthology*, available from Roger Dean Publishing Company (30/1838R).

The Subdivided Three and Four Patterns
Nine Pattern

Symphony No. 1 in C minor, op. 68, Movement 1	Johannes Brahms
Prelude to *Parsifal*	Richard Wagner
"She's Like the Swallow"*	George Mabry

Subdivided Three Pattern

Overture to *Prometheus*, op. 43, "Adagio"	Ludwig van Beethoven
Leonore Overture No. 3, op. 72b, "Adagio"	Ludwig van Beethoven
Overture to *Egmont*, op. 84	Ludwig van Beethoven

Twelve Pattern

St. Matthew Passion, "Aria," No. 47	J. S. Bach
Requiem in D minor, K.626, "Lacrymosa"	W. A. Mozart
Prélude à l'après-midi d'un faune	Claude Debussy

Subdivided Four Pattern

Messiah, "Surely He hath borne our griefs"*	G. F. Handel
Suite No. 3 in D, "Air"	J. S. Bach
Overture to *The Creation*	Franz Joseph Haydn
Mass No. 2 in G major, D.167, "Agnus Dei" and "Sanctus"*	Franz Schubert
"Adoro te Devote"*	arr. Stephen Caracciolo

The Six Pattern

Cantata No. 11, *Lobet Gott in sein en Reichen*, "Chorale"	J. S. Bach
Symphony No. 38 in D major, K.504, Movement 3	W. A. Mozart
Symphony No. 96 in D major, *The Miracle*, Movement 2	Joseph Haydn
Mass No. 2 in G major, D.167, "Benedictus"*	Franz Schubert
"Lord, Thy Help I Seek and Pray For," from *Drei Geistliche Leider**	Felix Mendelssohn
Symphonie Fantastique, op. 14a, Movement 3	Hector Berlioz
Elijah, op. 70, "Arioso"	Felix Mendelssohn
Variations on a Theme by Haydn, op. 56a, Variation VII	Johannes Brahms
Nuages	Claude Debussy
"Dide ta Deo"*	Uzee Brown, Jr.

The One Pattern

Gloria in D major, RV 589, "Qui sedes ad dexteram"*	Antonio Vivaldi
Fantasia for piano, chorus, and orchestra, *Choral Fantasy*, op. 80, "Presto"	Ludwig van Beethoven
Symphony No. 5 in C minor, op. 67, Movement 1	Ludwig van Beethoven
Symphony No. 7 in A major, op. 92, Movement 3	Ludwig van Beethoven
Emperor Waltz, No. 1	Johann Strauss
L'Arlésienne Suite, No. 2, II. "Menuet"	Georges Bizet
Symphony No. 9 in B-flat major, op. 83, Movements 2 and 4	Ludwig van Beethoven
Piano Concerto, No. 2, Movement 2	Johannes Brahms
Enigma Variations, op. 36, Variation 4	Edward Elgar
"En Ego Campana"*	Jacob Handl
"Fantasia on a Ukrainian Carol"*	arr. William Cutter

Continued on next page…

Irregular Meters
Five Pattern

Tristan and Isolde, Act 3, Scene 2	Richard Wagner
The Pines of Rome, Part II	Ottorino Respighi
Second Essay for Orchestra	Samuel Barber
Salome, Scene 1	Richard Strauss
"Gloria of the Angels"*	Douglas E. Wagner
"She's Like the Swallow"*	George L. Mabry

Seven Pattern

The Rite of Spring, "Spring Round Dances" in Part 1, and Part 2 (all)	Igor Stravinsky
Second Essay for Orchestra	Samuel Barber
"Hodie Christus"*	Taras Nahirniak

Uneven Two and Three Patterns
Fives

The Rite of Spring, "Games of the Rival Tribes" in Part 1, and Part 2 (all)	Igor Stravinsky
L'histoire du soldat (The Soldier's Tale), Scene 1	Igor Stravinsky

Sevens

The Firebird Suite	Igor Stravinsky
L'histoire du soldat (The Soldier's Tale), Scenes 1 and 2	Igor Stravinsky
Concerto for Piano and Orchestra, Movement 1	Aaron Copland
"Rejoice in the Lamb"	Benjamin Britten
Medea's Meditation and Dance of Vengeance, op. 33	Samuel Barber

Appendix E

Resources for Researching Credible Sources

Apel, Willi, ed. *Harvard Dictionary of Music.* Cambridge, MA: Belknap Press, 1977.

A-R Editions, Madison, Wisconsin. Recent Researches Series.

Blume, Friedrich, ed. *Das Chorwerk.* Wolfenbuttel: Moseler, 1956.

Crabtree, Phillip D., and David H. Foster. *Sourcebook for Research in Music.* Bloomington, IN: Indiana University Press, 1993.

Directory of Music Research Libraries. Repertoire international des sources musicales (RISM) ser. C. [2nd ed., rev. and enl.] Kassel: Barenreiter, 1983.

Dissertation Abstracts International. Ann Arbor, Michigan. University Microfilms, 1938. (Also available on CD-ROM.)

Donington, Robert. *The Interpretation of Early Music.* New rev. ed. New York: W. W. Norton, 1989. First published in 1963.

Duckles, Vincent H. and Michael A. Keller. *Music Reference and Research Materials: An Annotated Bibliography.* 4th ed. New York: Schirmer Books, 1993. First published in 1964.

Edwards, Warwick. "Sources of Instrumental Ensemble Music to 1630." *The New Grove Dictionary of Music and Musicians.* Vol. 17, pp. 702-17.

Ewerhart, Rudolf. *Cantio Sacra: Geistliche Solokantaten.* Cologne: Edmund Bieler, 1958.

Heyer, Anna Harriet. *Historical Sets, Collected Editions, and Monuments of Music: A Guide to Their Contents.* 3rd ed. 2 vols. Chicago: American Library Association, 1980. First published in 1957.

Marco, Guy A., ed. *Garland Composer Resource Materials.* New York: Garland Publications, 1981.

Phelps, Roger. *A Guide to Research in Music Education.* Metuchen: The Scarecrow Press, 1980.

Rilling, Helmuth. *The Discovery Series: Helmuth Rilling Master Class Lectures at the Oregon Bach Festival, 1979-1981 (Cantatas of J.S. Bach).* Transcribed by Marla Lowen. Dayton, OH: Roger Dean Publishing Company, 2000.

Ibid. 1982-1983, part I (Cantatas of J.S. Bach). Transcribed by Marla Lowen. Dayton, OH: Roger Dean Publishing Company, 2001.

Ibid. 1983, part II-1984 (Cantatas of J.S. Bach). Transcribed by Marla Lowen. Dayton, OH: Roger Dean Publishing Company, 2001.

Sadie, Stanley, ed. *The New Grove Dictionary of Music and Musicians.* London: Macmillan Publishers Ltd., 1985.

Westrup, Jack. *An Introduction to Music History.* 2nd ed. London: Jutchinson and Co. Ltd., 1973

Appendix F

Suggestions for Further Reading

Decker, Harold and Julius Herford. *Choral Conducting Symposium.* Englewood Cliffs, New Jersey: Prentice-Hall, 1988.

Frank, Milo O. *How to Run a Successful Meeting in Half the Time.* New York: Simon and Schuster, 1995.

Green, Elizabeth and Nicolai Malko. *The Conductor and His Score.* Englewood Cliffs, New Jersey: Prentice-Hall, 1975.

Green, Elizabeth. *The Modern Conductor.* Englewood Cliffs, New Jersey: Prentice-Hall, 1987.

Hustad, Donald and Kerchal Armstrong. *Choral Musicianship and Voice Training.* Carol Stream: Somerset Press, 1986.

Kahn, Emil. *Elements of Conducting.* New York: Schirmer Books, 1975.

Moe, Daniel. *Basic Choral Concepts.* Minneapolis: Augsburg Publishing House, 1972.

Rudolph, Max. *The Grammar of Conducting.* New York: Schirmer Books, 1950.

Webb, Guy, gen. ed., *Up Front! Becoming the Complete Choral Conductor.* Boston: E.C. Schirmer, 1993.

About the Author

Timothy W. Sharp is the Elizabeth G. Daughdrill Chair in the Fine Arts at Rhodes College, Memphis, Tennessee, and chairman of the Department of Music. He conducts the Rhodes Singers, MasterSingers Chorale and the Rhodes Orchestra, and teaches conducting. Dr. Sharp is equally at home on the podium for choral, operatic and orchestral performances. His ensembles tour on a regular basis and have established themselves as premiere artistic offerings.

In addition to *Precision Conducting* and *Achieving Choral Blend and Balance*, Dr. Sharp is a contributing author to *Up Front! Becoming the Complete Choral Conductor.* He has numerous compositions, recordings, articles, and paper presentations to his credit, and writes the featured column "Hallelujah!" for *Choral Journal.* He serves on the Editorial Board of the *Choral Journal* and the American Choral Directors Association Research and Publications Committee.

He holds MCM and DMA degrees from The School of Church Music, Louisville, Kentucky, and has completed further work in musicology at Harvard University and in orchestral conducting at the Aspen Music School.

Dr. Timothy W. Sharp

Dr. Sharp is indebted to his conducting teachers who have included J.P. Jardine, Jerry Warren, Richard Lin, Donald Hustad, Margaret Hillis, Fiora Contino, Martin Neary, and Jan Harrington.